ASHFOR

A HISTORY AND CELEBRATION
OF THE TOWN

LES LAWRIE

Produced by The Francis Frith Collection

www.francisfrith.com

First published in the United Kingdom in 2004 by
The Francis Frith Collection®

Hardback Edition 2004 ISBN 1-90493-806-x
Paperback Edition 2011 ISBN 978-1-84589-611-9

British Library Cataloguing in Publication Data

Ashford - A History and Celebration of the Town
Les Lawrie

The Francis Frith Collection®
Oakley Business Park, Wylye Road,
Dinton, Wiltshire SP3 5EU
Tel: +44 (0) 1722 716 376
Email: info@francisfrith.co.uk
www.francisfrith.com

Printed and bound in Great Britain
Contains material sourced from responsibly managed forests

Front Cover: **ASHFORD, BANK STREET c1950** A7101lt

Additional images and artwork by Les Lawrie
Domesday extract used in timeline by kind permission of Alecto
Historical Editions, www.domesdaybook.org.

Aerial photographs reproduced under licence from Simmons
Aerofilms Limited.
Historical Ordnance Survey maps reproduced under licence
from Homecheck.co.uk

*The colour-tinting in this book is for illustrative purposes only,
and is not intended to be historically accurate*

AS WITH ANY HISTORICAL DATABASE, THE FRANCIS FRITH ARCHIVE IS
CONSTANTLY BEING CORRECTED AND IMPROVED, AND THE PUBLISHERS
WOULD WELCOME INFORMATION ON OMISSIONS OR INACCURACIES

Contents

ASHFORD FROM THE AIR 1961 AFA95322

Historical Timeline for Ashford

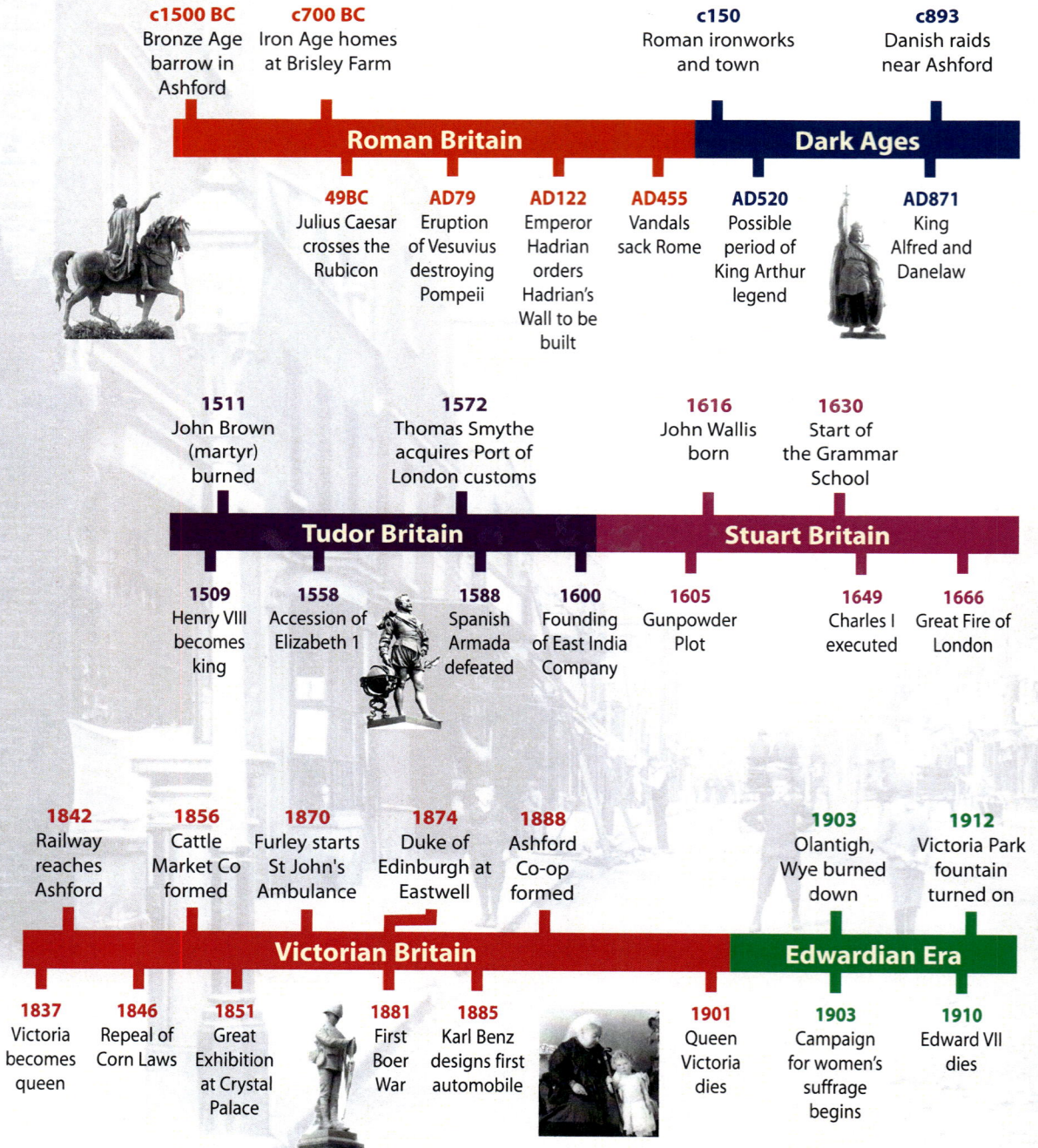

c1500 BC
Bronze Age barrow in Ashford

c700 BC
Iron Age homes at Brisley Farm

c150
Roman ironworks and town

c893
Danish raids near Ashford

Roman Britain

Dark Ages

49BC
Julius Caesar crosses the Rubicon

AD79
Eruption of Vesuvius destroying Pompeii

AD122
Emperor Hadrian orders Hadrian's Wall to be built

AD455
Vandals sack Rome

AD520
Possible period of King Arthur legend

AD871
King Alfred and Danelaw

1511
John Brown (martyr) burned

1572
Thomas Smythe acquires Port of London customs

1616
John Wallis born

1630
Start of the Grammar School

Tudor Britain

Stuart Britain

1509
Henry VIII becomes king

1558
Accession of Elizabeth 1

1588
Spanish Armada defeated

1600
Founding of East India Company

1605
Gunpowder Plot

1649
Charles I executed

1666
Great Fire of London

1842
Railway reaches Ashford

1856
Cattle Market Co formed

1870
Furley starts St John's Ambulance

1874
Duke of Edinburgh at Eastwell

1888
Ashford Co-op formed

1903
Olantigh, Wye burned down

1912
Victoria Park fountain turned on

Victorian Britain

Edwardian Era

1837
Victoria becomes queen

1846
Repeal of Corn Laws

1851
Great Exhibition at Crystal Palace

1881
First Boer War

1885
Karl Benz designs first automobile

1901
Queen Victoria dies

1903
Campaign for women's suffrage begins

1910
Edward VII dies

Middle Ages | Late Medieval

1086
Domesday Book lists Ashford

1282
Robert de Derby is first Rector

1424
Birth of John Fogge

1450
Jack Cade's Rebellion

1066
Battle of Hastings. Norman rule begins

1086
Domesday Book

1170
Murder of Thomas à Becket at Canterbury cathedral

1215
Magna Carta

1306
Robert the Bruce declares himself King of Scotland

1348
Black Death kills 25 million in Europe

1415
Battle of Agincourt

1485
Battle of Bosworth Field marks end of Plantaganet dynasty

Georgian Era

1756
Earthquake in Ashford

1797
First military garrison

1814
Fire Brigade acquire their first engine

1739
John Wesley founds Methodist church

1762
Mozart performs at the age of 6

1789
French Revolution

1815
Battle of Waterloo

1825
Stockton to Darlington Railway

20th Century Britain

1919
Mk IV tank arrives

1948
British Railways takes over railway works

1959
London overspill agreement

1974
Borough Council replace UDC

1994
Channel Tunnel opened

2003
High Speed Rail Link opened

1914
First World War begins

1926
John Logie Baird obtains first television picture

1939
Outbreak of Second World War

1956
Suez Crisis

1966
England win World Cup

1969
First man on the Moon

1982
Falklands Conflict

First Buildings and Re-buildings

FROM THE earliest times, people have been living in what is now Ashford. Evidence of Stone Age tools has been found in the vicinity. This is hardly surprising, since geographically Ashford lies at a natural crossroads. One route lies along the foot of the North Downs, the other goes through the Downs via the Stour valley gap (see below).

on the Downs nearby contains flints. There is therefore the possibility that tool-making was the first local industry in the area known as Ashford.

There is more definite evidence of Bronze Age occupation: barrows associated with that period have been found in Ashford and the surrounding area. Indeed, one barrow

THE STOUR GAP 2004 A71701k (Les Lawrie)

The ancient village of Wye is situated beside the River Stour at the entrance to the gap through the North Downs. The face of the downs at this side has a steep escarpment.

Although the Downs are not too difficult to scale, the human propensity for taking the easiest option indicates that early Britons would use these routes. Flints provided the key raw material for tools, and the chalk soil

was located in the north west part of the town, giving Barrow Hill its name. At this time trading became more important, so it is likely that relatively level routes would be the most used. The crossroads at Ashford would be a natural site for a settlement, especially with the availability of water from the River Stour nearby.

Recent excavations at Brisley Farm have uncovered evidence of extensive occupation of the site during the Iron Age. Any major new developments in and around Ashford require extensive and careful archaeological surveys before new buildings go up, indeed the survey at Brisley Farm has shown that Ashford has been a settlement for thousands of years. When Britain was part of the Roman Empire, two substantial roads crossed at Ashford. One was the road towards London from the port at Lympne (Lemanis) below the Downs escarpment, and the other led from the Weald of Kent and Sussex through Canterbury (Durovernum) to the major military base at Richborough (Rutupiae). A villa and a tomb were uncovered during the building of the Wall Estate and Albert Road, and a well was found near the churchyard. Both are close to the Roman road to Canterbury, but evidence of a complete small town was found at Westhawk, at the actual crossroads, in recent years.

ALBERT ROAD 1908 60326

A Roman villa was discovered when Albert Road was developed along with the Wall Estate.
Wall Road is the road to the right.

CANTERBURY ROAD 1908 60331x

The Roman road through Ashford to Canterbury went to the right of this one, and probably crossed it where the modern road bends to the right.

Did you know?

Vadum Fraxini

Ashford has had many names, but most have been more or less recognisable as Ashford. These have included Essetesford, Eshetisford, Ashetesford and Estefort, all meaning 'the ford near the ash trees'. If we translate this into Latin, 'Vadum Fraxini', this could possibly have been the name of our Roman town. If the crossroads had been more important than the ford, perhaps the name might have been 'Quadrivium Fraxini'.

Just outside the town wall, to the west, is an area that has now been identified as a very significant industrial area. Here iron was produced. The iron ore was mined in the Weald and transported along the road to Ashford, where large quantities of local charcoal would be used to turn the ore into workable metal. This was carried out using a range of furnaces. The iron then would be beaten on a form of anvil–a process which makes it into a more malleable metal. This process produces large quantities of hammerscale, and enough of this has been found to confirm the area in which the anvil stood.

ARTIST'S IMPRESSION OF THE ROMAN TOWN AND IRONWORKS DISCOVERED AT WESTHAWK
ZZZ00271 (Les Lawrie)

There were at least two iron works here over a long period of time, and sufficient iron was produced to leave nearly two tonnes of slag uncleared. The Roman roads in Kent would have suffered constant wear from regular traffic travelling through Kent to and from the continent, so most of the slag could have been used to repair those roads. This makes Ashford an early industrial town. Very little worked iron was found on the site, so most of the metal produced here would have been destined for use by the Roman army. The Roman practice was to have cemeteries outside the town walls, and such a cremation cemetery has been found in the excavations at the adjacent Brisley Farm site. All the evidence points to a substantial town on the site for a very long time.

The period from the end of the Roman Empire until the arrival of the Normans is very confused historically. This is partly because very little evidence remains from that time, and partly because the times were actually very confused, with many migrations, invasions and raids from outside the area. There are reports of raids at Great Chart and Appledore in about 893, when the escaping inhabitants fled to Ashford. Presumably, having had their homes sacked by Scandinavian raiders, these survivors would have been glad to receive the hospitality in Ashford and the chance to re-establish their

GREAT CHART, THE VILLAGE 1908 60339

Chart Magna was an important settlement, but it lacked Ashford's natural geographic advantages. There is no definite proof that it was sacked by the Danes.

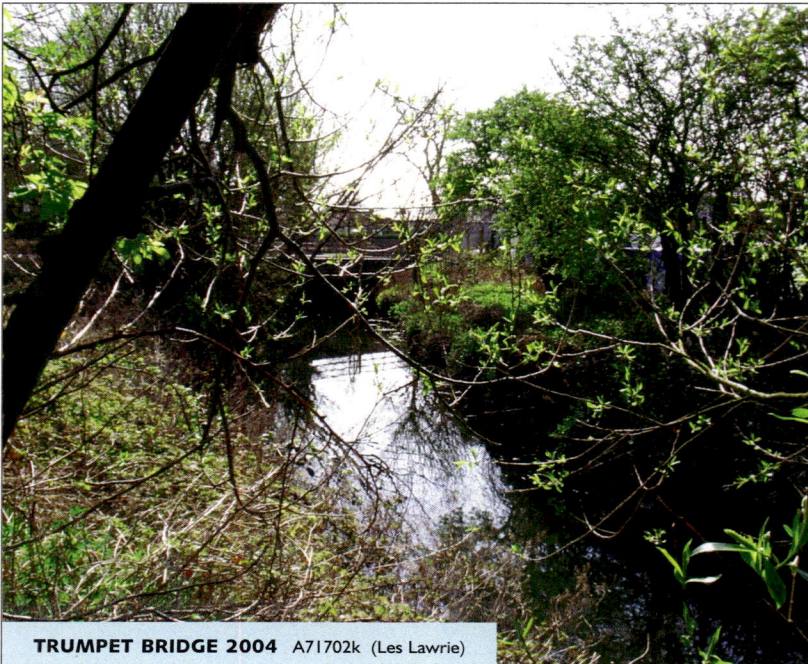

TRUMPET BRIDGE 2004 A71702k (Les Lawrie)

One clear piece of evidence of there being a Saxon settlement here is the very name Ashford. The first documented names are Essetesford or Eshetisford, which are of Saxon origin, meaning 'ford by the ash trees'. There has been considerable debate about exactly where the ford would have been, but I agree with Ruderman that it would have been on the Great Stour near Trumpet Bridge in Beaver Road (A71702k). Trumpet Bridge, the most likely site for the ash ford, is now a short bridge on raised banks either side of a small river. However, the area still flooded until quite recently.

The arrival of William the Conqueror and his Normans in Kent was less disruptive than in other parts of Britain, since the people of Kent appear to have negotiated their transfer of allegiance rather than be defeated. This gave Kent the right to use the motto 'Invicta', meaning 'unconquered'.

The first action by the Normans that many residents would have noticed would possibly have been the royal census of all land and property, the Domesday Book. This was conducted in 1085 and 1086 on the instructions of King William, and several parts of modern Ashford are surveyed: Ashford had land for 4 ploughs, a church with a priest, and 2 mills and was valued at 100 shillings; South Ashford had land for 1 plough, and 8 acres of meadow and was valued at 30 shillings (20 shillings before 1066); Essella had land for 1½ ploughs, and 6 acres of meadow and was valued at 20 shillings. Repton, Kennington and Eastwell are also listed.

From this it is clear that the collection of settlements that make up Ashford today all existed as Domesday manors. Some of today's manor houses can be seen as direct successors, though they are not necessarily on exactly the same site. The original Eastwell manor is more likely to be Lake House (see page 16), with the modern building being a replacement once the old one was no longer grand enough for the owners. Lake House is considered to be a 13th-century building with evidence for some earlier building.

REPTON MANOR HOUSE 2004 A71703k (Les Lawrie)

Repton Manor House served as a farmhouse until it was taken over by the Army in the Second World War. It probably stands on the site of the Fogge manor.

KENNINGTON, THE VILLAGE 1901 47540X

The forge, where the cart stands, is still used for metalworking by the Beresford family.

EASTWELL, THE CHURCH AND THE LAKE 1901 47539X

Lake House (right) is one of the oldest houses in the area; it was probably the original manor house. The churchyard contains the grave of Richard Plantagenet.

Ashford's church, mentioned in Domesday, was almost certainly replaced with a much more substantial stone structure in the early 13th century. The first recorded rector, Robert de Derby, was appointed in 1282. His portrait (see below) is thought to be one of the oldest church brasses in the country. The list of priests in charge of St Mary's Church (they were vicars from 1379) can be seen in the church.

Who is This?

This church brass, considered to be one of the oldest church brasses in Britain (some even think it is the oldest) is in Ashford parish church. It may picture the last unrecorded priest or Robert de Derby, the first recorded rector of Ashford (later, the priests in charge were vicars). He arrived in 1282, and was succeeded by William de Lucy in 1316. Many more elaborate church brasses can be found, some are also very old, but are there any as old as this small one? Notice the smooth outline of the top of the head. This is probably a tonsure, the shaven part of a monk's head, though it could just be that any lines were worn off. If the person represented was regarded as extremely pious or even saintly, many pilgrims would touch a particular part of the picture. This was in the hope of some good qualities rubbing off onto them. Thus, if thousands of people touched the top of the head of this brass, the lines cut in the brass would be rubbed off. However, since the outline still exists, this is unlikely.

Artist's Impression of a Church Brass in Ashford Parish Church ZZZ00272 (Les Lawrie)

Wool smuggling from Britain to the continent probably started around 1300 when Edward I imposed the first British customs duty. Since a market had been allowed at Ashford under a charter in 1243, some of the sales of sheep and wool would almost certainly have been for onward sale on the continent. Eventually the majority of the population between Ashford and the coast of the Romney Marsh were involved in smuggling. (The smuggling of brandy and lace from the continent only came about later, when custom duties were levied on these, and the smugglers, being good businessmen, realised that they could make good use of their return journeys). The livestock market, which may have been a centre for this trade, still operates in Ashford, and is one of the largest and most successful in Britain.

What a Shambles

The area around Middle Row in the High Street was a market area in medieval times. It probably started as a set of stalls selling meat and other foodstuffs; the meat would have been slaughtered very close by. A market like this was called a shambles. A gable end of one building decorated with a butcher's sign from 1659 still exists - indeed, the biggest collection of old buildings in the town is to be found around this area. The building currently occupied by Wards the estate agents has been identified as a probable market hall at some time; another possible site for a market hall is

Artist's Impression of Ashford Market Hall ZZZ00272 (Les Lawrie)

where Kings Parade is now. The market hall would also have covered an open area, which was probably the corn-market. The butter-market was at the High Street entrance to St John's Lane, which has buildings over it today - it would probably have been where the bingo club is now. There was also a fish market nearby. As we can see from the photograph, the Lower High Street in 1901 (47522x p.18-19) was still dominated by the former Market Hall behind the cart.

ASHFORD, HIGH STREET 1901 47522x

THE HARE AND HOUNDS, POTTERS CORNER 2004 A71704k (Les Lawrie)

The Hare and Hounds public house now stands at Potters Corner; note the toll collector's cottage at the entrance to Sandyhurst Lane.

During the 13th and 14th centuries there was a large amount of pottery produced in the vicinity of Potters Corner. Sufficient waste was uncovered to indicate positively that production was on an industrial scale. The pottery produced was distinctive, although similar to that produced at Tyler Hill in Canterbury. The name Potters Corner probably derives from this industry, either directly, or from a local family named Potter, whose ancestors had gained their name from their trade in this area.

There is little or no mention of Ashford in the reports of the Peasant's Revolt of 1381, although two men with Ashford connections, John Henwode and Stephen Repton, were charged with offences in Boughton Aluph and Wye. However, the grievances at the root of the revolt were still largely unaddressed by 1450.

Jack Cade is credited variously as being from Essex, Ireland or Ashford, but the strongest case seems to be for Ashford. In 1450, he led the opposition against corrupt Royal officials, and he actually had the support of many respectable middle-class people. It is believed that he gathered his local support together on Hothfield Common (above), taking them on for the mass gathering at Penenden Heath, Maidstone. Cade's forces met and defeated Royalist forces near Sevenoaks, and from there the revolt went on to London, where the Sheriff of Kent and others were captured and executed by the mob.

The heads of the Archbishop of Canterbury and the Lord Treasurer were arranged on top of two poles so they were 'kissing' each other. Further fighting followed, which ended in a stalemate.

HOTHFIELD, ON THE COMMON 1921 70317

Imagine hundreds of peasants, and others, gathering on the Common, ready to march on London with Jack Cade.

During a truce, Cade presented a list of grievances:

The King's closest advisors are totally dishonest;

The King is not above the law since he swore to uphold it;

Allegations of a Yorkist plot being involved are false;

Property is seized supposedly in the name of the King without payment;

The King cannot be seen without payment of a bribe;

Honest people are being labelled traitors so that the King's friends may enrich themselves;

The King's debts are not being paid;

Bribery and corruption is the norm in the judicial system, not justice;

The people of Kent have been taxed into poverty;

Corrupt people in public service should be dealt with through proper legal processes;

The King should unite the country and get rid of those who keep the Wars of the Roses going;

That the literate people of Kent should have some say in the government.

The King offered pardons to all but the leaders, which were accepted. The vast majority dispersed back to their homes, while the new Sheriff of Kent was sent to arrest Jack Cade. He was eventually run to earth in Hothfield, where

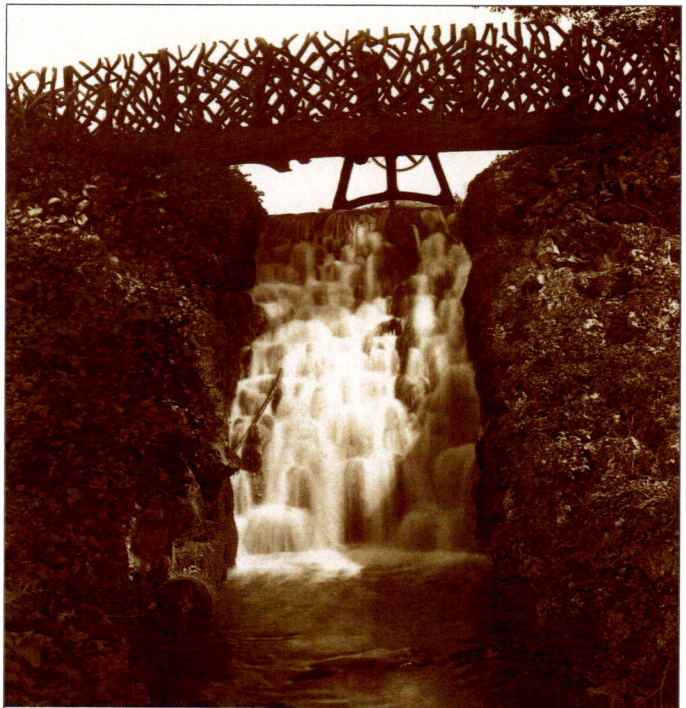

HOTHFIELD, THE WATERFALL 1901 47548

This waterfall is not too far from Rippers Cross farm, and may have supplied Jack Cade with water before his capture.

he was wounded - he died before he could be delivered to London for execution. Nevertheless, his body was hanged, drawn, and quartered and distributed around the kingdom as an example to others. Some authorities claim that Cade was caught at Heathfield (in Sussex), but in those days of non-standardised spelling, Hothfield could have been misread as Heathfield. Also, any person (or animal) seeking to avoid capture would generally choose their own home ground, where familiarity gives them an advantage. It is possible that Rippers Cross farm, Hothfield, derives its name from Jack Cade's capture.

One of the 'authorities' describing Jack Cade as an Ashfordian is none other than William Shakespeare in his history play 'Henry VI', part 2. He wrote the play in the late 16th century, considerably closer to the events and evidence than other accounts, so it is likely to be true - there was little for Shakespeare to gain from deliberate misrepresentation.

There is no written record of whether members of the Fogge family took part in the rebellion and were pardoned, or whether some betrayal of the trust of the local ex-soldier Jack Cade occurred. However, it was not uncommon for the wealthy to try to buy their way into heaven when they had a guilty conscience. They would do this through good deeds, generosity to the church, and paying for many masses to be said for their souls. Other motives could include rivalry, the 'keeping up with the Joneses' of that time. The Fogges were the prominent family in Ashford, while in nearby Wye the dominant family were the Kempes. In 1447, John Kempe had established a college for secular priests in his native Wye (see below). Its buildings are still used today to house part of Imperial College, London - the Latin School is the oldest part. Kempe became Chancellor of England, and a cardinal.

WYE, THE CHURCH FROM THE COLLEGE GARDENS 1960 W157045

Perhaps John Fogge, the lord of the manor of Repton, established his college of priests at Ashford following Kempe's example (see below); in much the same way, chantries were set up in other local churches (chantries were where choirs of monks would sing masses for the souls of their benefactors). The college, established in 1461, can still be seen today just east of the parish church, where it is the home of the parish priest. The northern wing has been removed, and the southern clad in brickwork, but the medieval timbered centre is still visible. The college was closed in 1536 at the time of Henry VIII's dissolution of the monasteries, though it may have been closed earlier on the death of Edward IV.

Isn't it Small for a College?

The residence for the vicars of Ashford is called The College, since it started out life as a college of priests, founded by John Fogge. The building has been divided into two, but still seems rather small to have been a college for training twelve priests. However,

Fogge's College

Artist's Impression of The College as originally built ZZZ00274 (Les Lawrie)

we find that Samuel Warren, vicar between 1673 and 1721, measured the rooms in the old building and described its layout. Enough of the original central portion remains to visualise its construction. From this an artist's impression has been created to show what it might have looked like when it was first built. The whole of the northern end was allowed to fall into decay, and was demolished in about 1765. At about this time the southern wing was clad in brickwork, and an extra wall was built in front to accommodate corridors and staircase, as they are today.

7th ASHFORD (S. Mary's) SCOUTS

present

FOGGE KNIGHT

An original comic Operetta

by

THE REVEREND D. P. LURY

in the

PARISH HALL, CHURCHYARD

Saturday, 22nd April, 1950

at 6.30 p.m.

Proceeds in aid of C. of E. Children's Society and
The Old People's Association

Admission by this Programme - Price 1/6

PROGRAMME FOR 'FOGGE KNIGHT' 1950
ZZZ00275 (From author's collection)

Programme for an operetta about John Fogge, founder of The College.

Did you know?

Why do Misericords Tilt?

In St Mary's Church there are twelve misericords of considerable age - these are seats which tilt up, revealing carving underneath. The up-tilted seat's top edge has a slight projection where a small adult may just rest their buttocks, while standing like a monk in a long service. However, if too much weight is put on these seats, they fall down with a crash! Is this to wake sleepy monks, or is it to inform their colleagues and embarrass the sleepy ones?

John Fogge certainly seems to have led an adventurous life - he supported several rebellions against the crown. He supported the Yorkist rebellion that gained Edward IV the crown, took part in the march of Fauconberg from Dover to release Henry VI from the Tower, and also later took part in the Duke of Buckingham's rebellion against Richard III, for which he was pardoned. He was lucky, for he benefited greatly from his part in these rebellions, holding high office under Edward IV (Treasurer and Comptroller of the Household) and another office in the reign of Henry VII.

He is credited with the considerable rebuilding work done on the parish church in the 1480s and 1490s, though it is probable that he was mainly the driving force (as well as a major contributor), getting all those with an interest to help. The first work was the erection of the tower, which was a squat affair until Sir John Fogge had it reinforced and raised to the current dominant height we see today (47524, p.26). Alterations to other parts of the church followed, such as the raising of the roof in the nave and chancel. It is strange that the windows in the tower were not blocked in when they no longer looked over the roof but under it - they look into the body of the church or the roof void. Fogge seems to have been the earliest in a chain of unconventional characters to be associated with Ashford in Tudor and Stuart times.

HIGH STREET AND THE CHURCH 1901 47524

Another interesting character whose lifespan bridges the gap between medieval and Tudor was a bricklayer at Eastwell Manor on the northern edge of the town. The records indicate that Richard Plantagenet, the last of the male line of that Royal house, died at the age of 81 in 1550. The story goes that he had watched the Battle of Bosworth, where his natural father, Richard III, lost his crown and died. Sensing that this was a possibility, Richard had ordered his son to keep out of the battlefield, and if all went badly to escape and conceal his parent's identity. This young Richard did, and travelling via London he eventually arrived at Eastwell, where he was employed as a bricklayer. His ability to read, extremely unusual in any but the highest strata of society, marked him out as very different. However, it appears that he was happy in his niche in the local community, and continued to enjoy the quiet life, with only one or two being told his story.

Can't the Builder See Straight?

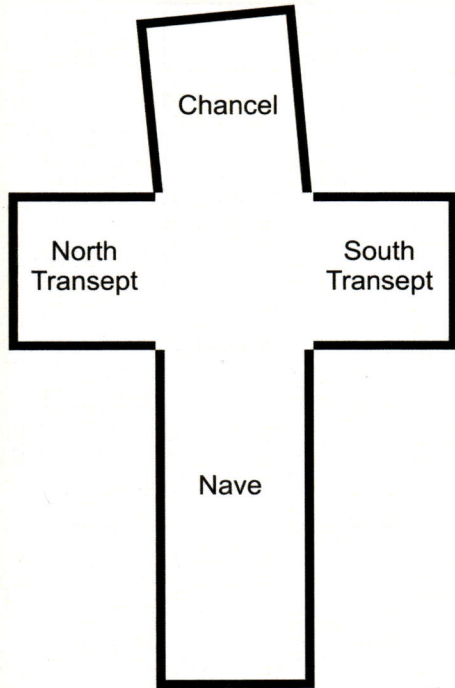

Diagrammatic Floor Plan of a Cruciform Church
ZZZ00277 (Les Lawrie)

Drawing of a Crucifix ZZZ00276 (Les Lawrie)]

The basic plan of many British churches is cruciform (in the shape of a cross). Some, like St Mary's, Ashford, have a modified form of cross shape: the chancel is not exactly in line with the nave, nor is it perpendicular to the transepts. The plan (ZZZ00277) shows that the head of the cross points slightly off to the left. Visitors to the church who look from the west door to the altar will see a diamond-pattern flagstone pavement running straight from them towards the altar. Looking more closely, they will see that it does not run straight down the centre aisle, but at a slight angle to it. Is this the result of careless workmanship, or perhaps a re-evaluation of the alignment of the church over the centuries? The most likely reason is that it reflects the traditional position of the head of Jesus in a crucifix, leaning slightly to the left (ZZZ00276).

CHAPTER TWO

Productive Nonconformism

ASHFORD gained a reputation in the 16th and 17th centuries for the nonconformism of its population. Questioning the established order has, historically, given us the Reformation, the emancipation of slaves, universal suffrage, and so on. New ideas have to come from somewhere; so Ashford should take a pride in its 'awkward squad'.

Early in the reign of Henry VIII, while he was still accepting the authority of the Pope in Rome, various 'heretic' Protestants were prosecuted, and some were executed. Among these was an Ashford cutler called John Brown. He was burned at the stake on Whit Sunday 1511 after a conversation that he had had with a friend from Rolvenden was reported to the authorities. (This John Brown precedes the other John Brown, whose body supposedly lies 'a-mouldering in his grave', according to the song. Who knows, perhaps the song already existed, and was merely revived at the beginning of the American Civil War? After all, the US national anthem used a London drinking club tune). Ashford's John Brown was executed at Martyrs' Field by the River Stour (see below). It later became unusual for people to be burned in their own town, in case a mob of their local friends decided to rescue them.

HENWOOD 2004 A71705k (Les Lawrie)

This is Martyrs' Field at the entrance to the Henwood industrial estate, site of the burning of 'heretics'. The building is the office of the charity Mission Aviation Fellowship.

By 1556 the religious cycle had again returned to Roman Catholicism under Queen Mary I. During the year a 'number of Kentish people' were executed by burning at Ashford, part of the purge against Protestants carried out at the behest of Mary. The identities of these martyrs are not known, but the following year two other men died at the stake. These were Matthew Bradbridge and Nicholas Final, who came from Tenterden. Their widows were later burned to death at Canterbury, and so were five men known to have come from Ashford: Humphrey Middleton, Richard Colliar, William Stere, Richard Wright and John Herst. John Brown's son Richard was only saved from the same fate as his father by the death of Queen Mary.

In about 1554, Thomas Smythe (see above) acquired the manor of Ashford as the dowry for his wife Alice Judde. Thomas was a customs official for Mary I, a position he purchased for £2500. He remained in his customs role through two changes of sovereign until eleven years into the reign of Elizabeth I. In 1567 the displeasure of the Queen was incurred when a shortfall of £6000 was identified in the issuing of privy warrants. Smythe survived this, thanks to friends in court.

He later persuaded the Queen that he

DRAWING OF SIR THOMAS SMYTHE AS PORTRAYED ON HIS TOMB ZZZ00278 (Les Lawrie)

Sir Thomas Smythe from his tomb

could 'farm' the customs duties of the ports of London, Sandwich and Chichester for a rent of £30,000 and other payments. Elizabeth kept an eye on the success of the project, and became unhappy whenever Smythe made too much profit. She then increased the annual payments accordingly. He was twice accused of bribery, and only survived by 'bribing' the Queen herself. His on-off relationship with Elizabeth I continued until his death in 1591, for he was also given two royal estates in Kent.

Customer Smythe, as he had become

THE PARISH CHURCH 1901 47528

We are looking at the south transept of St Mary's Church, the Strangford Smythe chapel. Ivy has been found to damage stonework, so it has since been removed from the building.

acknowledged. Smythe's tomb, the first of three Smythe family tombs in St Mary's Church (see this page), is certainly impressive. Without any other documentary evidence, it is possible to work out that he had thirteen children, one of whom died in infancy. The tomb depicts six sons, one of whom died young and before his father, so his sculpture carries a skull and does not have a beard. The six daughters all outlived him.

Another tomb in St Mary's is that of Sir Richard Smythe, Customer Smythe's fourth son. This is a fascinating illustration of the social history of the family. On the tomb three wives are depicted, two with the obligatory skull to show their having died before Sir Richard.

Some of the Church of England were turning towards more Puritan ideas during the reign of Elizabeth I. In 1581, Joseph Mynge was appointed vicar of Ashford, and he soon got into trouble with the Archbishop for refusing to accept his six articles - these articles were intended to enforce conformity within the Church of England, something that has never been easy to achieve. However, in 1584, before Mynge could be dragged before an ecclesiastical court, he died!

One of the earliest families to settle permanently in America was that of Francis

known, was a very active businessman. He was the banker for the Port of Dover, he had considerable interests in lead and copper mining, and he was an active and enthusiastic participant in the Virginia and Muscovy companies. Smythe had important connections with the foundation of the American colonies, which are rarely

Fashions from Long Ago

Drawing: Lady Smythe 1
ZZZ00279 (Les Lawrie)

Drawing: Lady Smythe 2
ZZZ002880 (Les Lawrie)

Drawing: Lady Smythe 3
ZZZ00281 (Les Lawrie)

Fashion changes over the years, and the styles of clothes we wear can change slightly or even radically. To find out what people wore some time ago, we need to look at whatever records there are. Since original pattern books for the period do not exist, we need other sources. These are almost always portraits or sculptures of the wealthy - ordinary people were hardly ever portrayed. St Mary's Church has elaborate sculptures on the tombs of members of one wealthy local family, the Smythes.
Sir Richard Smythe's tomb is particularly interesting, for it has sculptures of his three wives. Note that his first wife wears a ruff around her neck, a particular style of scarf and what seems to be a plain gown. The second wife still has the ruff, but has flowers decorating her hair and a blouse under her dress. His third wife appears to be wearing a great deal of lace on her collar, her bonnet and around the shoulders of her dress.

and Marie Epps. They settled in Virginia early in the 1600s, at a place called Appomattox Manor, by the James River near Ashford's twin town of Hopewell. Part of the plantation remained in the family's ownership until the late1970s, when it was acquired by the National Park service. Appomattox achieved even more historical significance in the 1800s with the close of the American Civil War. Francis Epes (Epps) was born in North Street (see page 34 - the house is now occupied by Clague, the architects, and a builder) at the beginning of 1597, but by 1625 he was well established as a leading citizen in Virginia - he was elected to the local assembly. He returned to Britain for an extended visit, during which one his children was born in 1630. Epps lived well past sixty years old, and was survived by his children, including his sons Thomas and Francis.

1616 is a date that is celebrated worldwide, but hardly known about in Ashford. Yet the birth of the vicar's son, John Wallis, in that year gave Ashford its greatest intellect ever. John Wallis was sent off to school in Tenterden in 1625 to avoid the plague which had broken out in Ashford. John proved a brilliant scholar, being ready for university by the age of 13. Felsted School gave him the necessary grounding in classical languages and logic, but he also discovered mathematics through his brother, and this was to change his life.

In 1637 be gained a BA, in 1640 an MA, and he was ordained. Whilst a chaplain he discovered an ability in cryptography, which he then used 'on behalf of the parliamentary party'. After his marriage in 1645, Wallis met weekly with other leading scientists in London - this group became the Royal Society in 1660. This discussion of ideas and reading nurtured his love of mathematics, and he developed his own ideas.

Wallis published several books paving the way for modern mathematics. He was appointed to the Savilian Chair of geometry at Oxford in 1649, mainly for his support of the Parliamentarians, but he held this chair until his death in 1703, and was confirmed in it by succeeding monarchs, because he deserved it for his scholarship. A political appointee he certainly was, but he deserved to hold the chair.

EPPS HOUSE, NORTH STREET 2004 A71739k (Les Lawrie)

Why Worry about Wallis?

The College, the vicar's home (below), was where John Wallis was born. His father died when John was only six years old. John Wallis was a contemporary at Emmanuel College with the John Harvard of Harvard University, and he was one of the main tutors of Isaac Newton. However, he must be considered for his own mathematical achievements. Why is John Wallis so important? The answer is that much of the basis of mathematics as we know it depends on ideas first published by Wallis. For instance, he realised that any number system must be complete to be used for serious mathematics;

BULL YARD 2004   A71738k (Les Lawrie)

The lane through Bull Yard may have been the route taken by John Wallis going to Tenterden. Bull Yard is named after the Pied Bull Inn to the left and overhead.

The College A71706k (Les Lawrie)

the Roman system of numbering fails, because it lacks a zero. In the 1600s, mathematicians had yet fully to define a number system, and Wallis was the first person to have a solution to the problem published. In 'Arithmetica Infinitorum', he developed the idea of infinity, and even designed its accepted symbol, a curve with no end (see below). Many modern ideas, not just in mathematics, science and economics, are represented in the form of formulae. Meanings of symbols must be consistent with every use; it was Wallis who published the first systematic use of formulae.

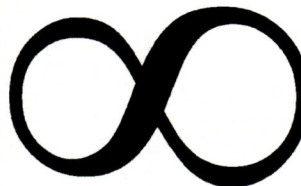

Wallis's Symbol for Infinity
ZZZ00282 (Les Lawrie)

A typical Ashfordian, Wallis did not even conform in his non-conformism, for he spoke out and signed a document against the execution of Charles I. This may account for his acceptance by Charles II, who even appointed him as a royal chaplain and then nominated him as a member of a committee to revise the Church of England prayer book.

He wrote many other books on religion, grammar, and logic, and even devised a system for teaching the deaf and dumb, but he is best known, perhaps, for his pupil, who gave all the credit to John Wallis for his mathematics and gravitational work - Isaac Newton. His contribution to mathematics is regarded as one of the essential precursors to today's information and communication technology.

In 1630, Sir Norton Knatchbull, a local gentleman and a former MP for Kent, founded a grammar school at the west end of the churchyard (A71075).

The first building for the school bears the date 1635, but nevertheless it is one of the oldest buildings constructed of brick without any other supporting framework. The building can still be seen, and it houses the Ashford

THE CHURCHYARD 1965 A71075

The school, now renamed the Norton Knatchbull School, is still in existence nearly 400 years later, though it has moved twice and has had a considerable amount of extra buildings erected (see page 38). The school is one of the oldest in the country. There were close ties with the parish church; one piece of evidence for this is the installation of a gallery in the church in 1637 for use by the Grammar School boys (shown right). The retention of galleries in a parish church is very unusual. St Mary's galleries are sometimes used, but they could not accommodate all the boys now at the school.

THE PARISH CHURCH, THE INTERIOR 1960 A71050

The Long-lived Norton Knatchbull

Norton Knatchbull, owner of Mersham-le-Hatch and some prosperous estates, was knighted in 1604. He entered parliament to represent Kent in 1609, but he is better known for founding Ashford Grammar School in 1630. His nephew, Norton, knighted in 1641, was created baronet. During the Civil War, he retired to Mersham and wrote 'Commentary on the New Testament', something of a standard academic text for the next two centuries. Norton became the name of choice and tradition for many of the eldest sons of the family. The ninth holder of the baronetcy was created Baron Brabourne in 1880. After an education reorganisation, Ashford Grammar School became the Norton Knatchbull School. In 1980, the 350th anniversary speech day attracted as guest speaker the world-famous Peter Ustinov. This meant national newspaper coverage, including the Daily Mirror, where a reader apparently commented that Norton Knatchbull was a silly name to call a school. Reputedly Lord Romsey, the eldest Knatchbull son, replied with the statement: 'I am Norton Knatchbull!'

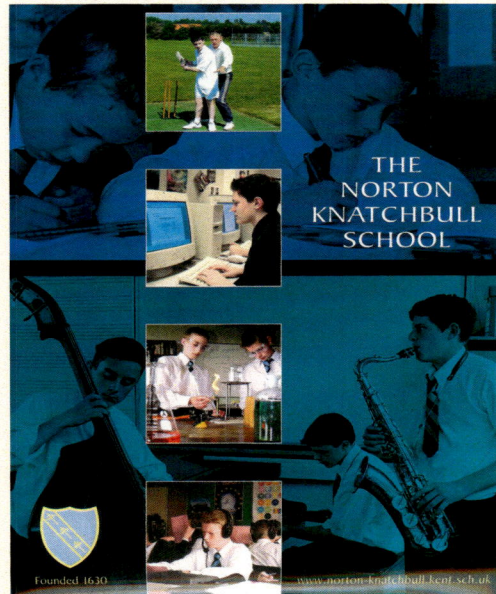

The Norton Knatchbull School,
Prospectus Cover ZZZ00283

ASHFORD GRAMMAR SCHOOL 1901 47531

These buildings, opened in a blizzard in 1881, ceased to be used by the school in 1958.

Another Ashford link with the American colonies was the Starr family. Thomas and Prudence Starr had fourteen children (or seventeen, according to one source), but some of their names seem strange to modern ears. Jehosaphat, Thomas, Comfort, Nostrength, Moregifte, William, Standwell and Joyfull were the boys, while the girls were Judith, Suretrust, Mercy, TruthShallPrevayl (Truthful or Veritas), Constante, Anne, Mary and Beloved. Jehosaphat, Thomas, Comfort, Moregifte, Joyfull, Suretrust and Constante survived beyond childhood and married. Two of the boys achieved fame: one, Comfort, after he had been a churchwarden of the parish church, and the other, Joyfull, while he held that office. Dr Comfort Starr lived in the lower High Street and practiced as a chirurgeon (the equivalent of a surgeon), dispensing medical treatment to ordinary people, as opposed to a physician, whose main clients would be the gentry. Dr Starr was clearly a prominent citizen, with an estate in Ashford, which he passed to his son Comfort in his will.

As a man of standing in the community he took a significant part in the activities of the parish church, and in 1631 he was elected warden. In 1634 a committee for repairs on the church of St. Mary included

2

Since the name Elizabeth Starr is not listed as emigrating with her husband, it is generally assumed that she followed later. Another explanation is that since a wife was her husband's chattel, or property, she went with him to America unrecorded. Presumably any daughters would have been treated the same way. So it could just have been that Dr Starr was just plain dishonest, in the modern way of assessing honesty, in hiding his women's presence on the 'Hercules'. Many left Britain for America without declarations being made.

Once in New England, Dr Starr acquired a house at New Towne (now Cambridge, Massachusetts), and restarted his work in medicine. He is chiefly remembered in the United States for his part in the founding of America's oldest University College, Harvard. Some reports state that Harvard Yard is sited in what was the front yard of the Starr farm.

During the improvements carried out at the time of Sir John Fogge, an altar was erected at the east end of the parish church. This was an elaborate altar with an impressive inscription:

Altare Dei Decoratur,
Vestibulum ditans, & plura Iocalia Donans,
Ut patet intuitu, pro Posteribus memoranda
Ad Laudem Domini, cui Laus sit nunc & in dvum.
Amen.

Warren, in his history of Ashford Parish, tells how he looked at the stonework around Sir John Fogge's tomb and came to the conclusion that there had been a series of steps leading up to the dominating high altar. This altar was still in the church in the early

1600s, when Ashford became increasingly led by Puritans. Eventually, during the unsettled times of the Civil War, the Puritans gained control of the parish church.

One Puritan belief was that the words of the Bible were to be followed literally, if possible. The second commandment was applied to any sculpture or picture, and especially those in churches: 'Thou shalt not make unto thee any graven image, or any likeness of any thing that is in heaven above, or that is in the earth beneath, or that is in the water under the earth: thou shalt not bow down thyself to them, nor serve them: for I the Lord thy God am a jealous God, visiting the iniquity of the fathers upon the children unto the third and fourth generation of them that hate me: and shewing mercy unto thousands of them that love me, and keep my commandments'. Perhaps the Puritans of Ashford felt offended by the imagery in the church.

John Maccuby, vicar of Ashford, was removed from his office by the congregation and replaced by a Presbyterian, Joseph Boden, in 1643. He was clearly a prominent Puritan in Kent, since he preached to the County Committee. The following year, Joy Starr (some sources say his name was Joyfull, while others give Joyfoole or even O Be Joyful as his baptismal name) and William Worsley were the churchwardens of the parish church. These two leading local Puritans then deliberately destroyed the altar and altar-piece. Other damage done at about the same time included the smashing of the heraldic glass that was then in the west window of the church - presumably this was done using guns.

It has to be assumed that Starr and Worsley felt pride in what they had done, since they had their names carved in a stone plaque, which was inset about 5 or 6 feet above the floor level in the east wall of the parish church. It has been alleged that other materials were taken for their own private use, such as building materials. Warren's history reports that he remembers the removal of the plaque from the wall. He describes a local lawyer, named Marsh, getting considerable pleasure from completely removing the carved inscription.

Altar rails at this time were often burned, but Ashford's escaped. They were reclaimed in about 1697, the time that the new altar was erected. The rails then served several purposes around the church. For instance, when the archbishop or the archdeacon visited the parish church, the rails were used for keeping the ordinary people in their place, the equivalent of modern crowd control barriers.

Starr and Worsley also managed to establish some useful items. In the space at the east end of the church where the altar had been destroyed by this infamous pair, benches were placed against the wall. These were later used in the vestry, together with the communion table, which also survived for a useful purpose - the benches and table were used by parishioners for their meetings. Obviously the later church leaders took a more practical view of what had been done, rather than undo absolutely everything that had been done just as a matter of principle. An altar and altar-piece were rebuilt after the money was raised though public subscription, which started in 1695.

There are other ecclesiastical reminders of this turbulent time in Ashford's history. Ashford Baptist Church was founded in 1653, and its impressive façade still looks out on Station Road, once Marsh Street (see below). In 1662 the Act of Uniformity was used to force the Puritan Nicholas Prigg out of the parish church, so he started the Ashford Congregational Church. The last separate Congregational church building was demolished to make way for the magistrates' court in the 1970s.

Recognised now as the earliest professional woman writer, Aphra Behn was born locally in about 1640. She is believed to have lived in Wye, close to Ashford, at some stage in her colourful career. During her early life she somehow became literate, which was not the norm for ordinary people in 17th-century England. Suggestions that her father was a simple barber seem implausible, unless he also practised as a chirurgeon - these two occupations were often combined! Aphra certainly become well educated, because she was able to carry out translations from French and Latin into English.

About 1663 she travelled to the Dutch colony of Surinam, where her experiences provided source material for one of her best-known works, the novel 'Oroonoko, or the History of the Royal Slave', published in 1688. This book was one of the earliest to portray Africans, and especially African slaves, with sympathy. These were not to be the last controversial views from Mrs Behn.

She had become Mrs Behn on her return from Surinam, probably stopping off at the new colony of Virginia, where the Epps family from Ashford were by then well established. Mr Behn is variously believed to have been a merchant, a mariner or even to have been dreamed up to make Aphra a widow and hence respectable. Whoever Mr Behn was, he was only 'on the scene' for a very short time, and Aphra never married again.

She next pops up in Antwerp, where she was acting as a spy for the

MARSH STREET 1903 50330

Marsh Street has now become Station Road, and the only building remaining from those in this view is the Baptist Church. Many of the rest went to make room for the Ringway.

British government. This seems to have triggered her writing career, since the British government were very tardy in paying Aphra for her work. She got so far into debt that creditors were threatening her with prison, and in order to make a living, she therefore turned to writing professionally. Her writing career produced at least 15 novels, though these were much shorter than the novels of today. She also published translations, and she was a successful playwright: she wrote 17 or more plays, including 'The Forc'd Marriage' (1670), 'The Rover' (1677), 'Sir Patient Fancy' (1678), 'The Roundheads' (1681), and 'The City Heiress' (1682). Many of these plays were comedies.

Aphra's life and work appear to have been a reaction to the recently ended Puritan rule of Cromwell and the Commonwealth. She was typical of the time in that her style of writing is lively, even bawdy, with a great deal of sexual innuendo. Other writers of the period found difficulty coping with the idea that a woman could be a successful writer. They accused her of plagiarising work and of using male ghost writers, among other things. These attacks made her one of the earliest feminists, with a consciousness of the female condition.

Women were not supposed to be able to compete in a man's world, though Aphra did, and did so successfully. Her work was attacked because she wrote openly about human sexuality. These ideas were also being portrayed by male writers of the time, but the suspicion has to be that many were jealous of Aphra Behn's success. At least now her ability to write is fully recognised, in contrast to the bigoted attacks that were made throughout her writing career.

Godinton House (see below), built in the 17th century, was home to many generations of Tokes. The last owner left the house to a charitable trust so that it would be looked after for years to come. The most well-

GODINTON HOUSE 1901 47562

known Toke was Captain Nicholas Toke, who gave the house its unique decorations. In the wooden panelling there are carved figures carrying out pike and musket drill - many of the drills are continued today by the Honourable Artillery Company. Captain Toke led a full active life, outliving five wives. He was apparently making his way to London to find a sixth wife when he died. He was only 93!

Troops had been stationed in Ashford during the Civil War, and on and off there were troops quartered here for most of the 18th century. A report of 1698 mentions their main role: this was not defending the country against foreign invaders, but trying to prevent smuggling, especially of wool. Getting any action taken against the smugglers must have been extremely difficult, since prominent citizens were often involved in the trade.

One example of this is a doctor called Isaac Rutton, who lived in a house on what is now the corner of the High Street and Bank Street (A71011). He was a respected local physician, who had married into the Toke family of Godinton House, and he was a Justice of the Peace. However, he was also the leader of the Seasalter Company of smugglers. He had sons who lived in Badlesmere and Ospringe (at least one of them was a parson), and they were thought to operate staging points for the gang.

Otherwise, the 1700s in Ashford appear to have been a time when small local events were the norm. Several occurrences are worthy of note, however. For instance, natural phenomena are not frequent in Ashford, so a subterranean fire that burned for some time under several acres of land at Hinxhill in 1727 must have created quite a stir. On 1 June 1756 there was an earthquake in the area, which was recorded as being accompanied by a noise 'as if a wagon was passing'.

Some people come to Ashford, do a good job, and pass on, but they are not noticed until many years later. One such person arrived in 1774: the vicar. He was not succeeded until 1826, making his incumbency about 52 years. This Mr Bond, James Bond, is probably only noticed because he shares a name with the hero of many books written by the 20th-century author, Ian Fleming. Ian Fleming was also a man with local connections. Did he subconsciously note the name on a visit to Ashford, and then later immortalise James Bond in his novels?

Did you know?

Smuggling Gangs

During the 1700s and 1800s there were many gangs of smugglers operating in and around Ashford. Some were known by the home village of some of their members. These included the Aldington Gang, also called the Blues, led by George Ransley from Ruckinge. The Seasalter Company had some very wealthy leaders - in 1812, one left over a million pounds in his will. Most notorious was the Hawkhurst Gang, though they actually worked once with the Wingham Gang.

KENT COUNTY MAP SHOWING ASHFORD AND SURROUNDING AREAS c1850

CHAPTER THREE

Garrison Town, Railway Town and Market Town

MAGAZINE ROAD 1908 60329

Magazine Road was only developed on the one side we see here. The land opposite the houses was an open space, later a cricket ground; maybe that is where the boys in the photograph have been.

ASHFORD REALLY started to grow as a town when the British Army established a garrison at Barrow Hill in 1797. At the time there were only about 300 houses in the town, so a complete army unit would have made a huge impact. Proper barracks were built in 1805, and they continued in use until the end of the Napoleonic Wars. At their height they housed a garrison of troops who outnumbered the local population. The barracks probably stood on the site now occupied by St Mary's Primary School, since a well existed here in the early 20th century, which would have provided water for the troops. The well was very useful to the allotment holders, but it was much older than the allotments.

Did you know?

Not every Magazine Contained Explosives

Magazine Road (see left) commemorates one of the magazines built by the army on the road leading from Barrow Hill toward Canterbury. Generally, when we talk about a magazine (in the military sense), we mean a powder magazine. This specialised use of the word has developed. Magazines were basically just storerooms, and this one in Ashford was a store for foodstuffs such as biscuit. Service personnel relied on a hard biscuit as food, because it lasted a long time without becoming too rotten to eat!

Following the downfall of Napoleon, the army was drastically cut down in size. The barracks at Barrow Hill were demolished, and many soldiers returned to their home towns, including Ashford, for some of the soldiers would have made local connections and decided to move to this area rather than return to their birthplaces. This number of returning ex-servicemen clearly placed a strain on the resources of the town, since a report of 1818 commented that the population of 2500 included many unemployed ex-servicemen.

Ashford had clearly been identified as a town of strategic importance in the event of any invasion from the continent of Europe.

The result of this was that troops would be based in Ashford on and off until the late 20th century. The transfer of the Intelligence Corps base, together with the closure of the Rowcroft workshops, ended the stationing of regular forces in the town after more than two centuries. The buildings in Barrow Hill Terrace (see page 51), Barrow Hill Cottages and Barrow Hill Place (see below) have long been thought to have been Victorian barracks - Barrow Hill Place was possibly the officers' quarters. This is supported by the discovery some years ago of a blacksmith's forge underneath a fireplace in a bungalow between the rows of buildings; this could have been the stables for the soldiers' horses.

BARROW HILL PLACE 2004 A71707k (Les Lawrie)

BARROW HILL TERRACE 2004
A71708k (Les Lawrie)

Barrow Hill Terrace is thought to have been part of the Victorian barracks. Behind is a row of smaller houses, Barrow Hill Cottages, where a plane crashed in the Second World War.

Fires and fire fighting were a private matter until well into the 1800s. If a property caught alight, it was up to the occupier alone, or with the help of the people in the immediate neighbourhood, to try to douse the fire. Some places had fire insurance, which could include the services of their private fire fighting teams. If there was no team available in your area, or if it was employed by a different fire insurance company, then you were on your own! At least one property in Middle Row had fire insurance, since there is a fire mark on it; though how the insurance company could fight a fire with no team of fire-fighters in Ashford is open to discussion.

Ashford was one of the earliest towns to develop a formal volunteer fire brigade, who would fight fires for all the citizens. By 1814 they were in a position to buy a fire 'engine', almost certainly little more than just a pump. Simon Bagg describes it as very simple, and needing to be moved on rollers from its store

at the west end of the parish church. He also reports an amusing incidence of the firemen commandeering a fish cart from a passer-by, loading the engine onto it, and getting to the fire much more quickly than they would otherwise have managed.

This volunteer fire brigade continued to operate independently until 1896 when they became part of the National Fire Brigade Service. The members took considerable pride in their work and independence, and in 1863 objected to the interference, as they saw it, of the newly formed local board.

Probably the most important event in the development of modern Ashford was the arrival of the railway in 1842. The town was now connected to the capital by a fast mass transport system. Other rail routes were opened in rapid succession - through Canterbury in1846, across Romney Marsh to Hastings in 1850 (by the Lord Mayor of London, no less!) and finally through Maidstone in 1884. This pattern of routes in five different directions is unusual in a town that was as small as Ashford. Four of the routes can be seen as resulting from Ashford's status as a railway town - or perhaps they were the cause of that status. These routes were part of the South Eastern Railway's network across the region, reinvigorating Ashford in its historic position as a strategic crossroads - in this case railroads!

Ashford gained its very tentative first toehold in the electronic age courtesy of the SER in 1845. This was the transmission of urgent messages using the telegraph. The messages would have to be really vital, because the cost per message was eight shillings and sixpence, more than many people earned in a week!

The other route, from Maidstone, was a result of a bitter feud between the railway companies: the builders, the London, Chatham & Dover Railway, even built their own terminus several hundred yards west of the existing Ashford Station. This station was only used by passengers for a few years; it was then bypassed and turned into a parcels depot. The feud had ended with the amalgamation of the two railway companies as the South Eastern & Chatham Railway. The success of the railway was quickly confirmed by the increased volumes of passenger and freight traffic through the station. The original station was unable to cope, and had to be rebuilt by 1865.

However, the SER had not only built a railway junction, but they had also decided that Ashford should be the site of a major works (see above). This complex just south of the line would be used to build locomotives and carriages. The railway works opened in 1847, the same year that the company started building a model village nearby to accommodate their employees. Model

THE CLOCK TOWER OF THE RAILWAY WORKS 2004 A71709k (Les Lawrie)

Positioned at the main gate, the clock would have encouraged prompt attendance at the works. The main buildings can be seen through the gate in the background.

villages were complete settlements, providing housing, work, shopping and leisure in a single community. These were provided, as a complete planned package, by the owners of the factory, mill, or in this case, railway works. Other examples of model villages can be found at Bourneville (for the Cadburys' chocolate factory), or New Lanark (for Robert Owen's mills).

This model village was originally called Alfred, but later became known as Newtown (see page 53). The houses surrounded a village green, and next to it were a shop, a public house and public baths. A school for the village was also provided. Few of the needs of the workers living there were not satisfied.

Newtown was the start of the rapid expansion to accommodate railway employees and those dependent on them for a livelihood. The development of South Willesborough followed soon after, starting in 1852. By 1864 about 3000 people were living south of the railway line; they were dependent largely on the SER, so much so that the company decided to build the Railwaymen's Church - Christchurch. The church was in use by 1867, though it is interesting to note that the Locomotive public house opposite the church opened the year before.

Did you know?
Couldn't run a Booze-up in a Pub

In Victorian times, it is generally believed, running a public house was a sure-fire way to success. This was not always the case! In 1853 the tenant of the Castle Inn, Philip Mein, was given notice to quit. He owed the brewery for the beer they had supplied, and they could not see him paying his debt, because of his mismanagement of the pub. He was advised to find a smaller house that his wife could manage.

NEWTOWN 2004 A71710k (Les Lawrie)

We are looking across the green of the model village towards the other amenities. The wheels commemorate the 150th anniversary of the arrival of the railway in 1992.

A succession of engineers took charge of the railway works; these engineers are best known for their influence on the locomotives built there. James Stirling, who had come to Ashford from Scotland in 1878, was so successful in producing powerful and attractive locomotives that he was awarded a gold medal at the 1889 Paris Exhibition for one of his express engines. The actual engine was one of the products of the Ashford works.

During this period many plans were floated for other railway lines, most of which were never started. One such was a line from Ashford through Tenterden and on to Lewes and Brighton. If this had come to fruition, imagine how it would fit into the rail system of today!

Why Stop at Dover?

The South Eastern Railway, having completed their rail network in Kent, started to look seriously at crossing the English Channel in comfort. In 1857 they had been made aware of the serious proposals of Thomé de Gamond for a rail tunnel joining France with Britain. After the Franco-Prussian war, the two governments agreed a joint scheme. Serious digging started in 1881, starting from the bottom of Shakespeare Cliff between Folkestone and Dover. This had reached just about a mile before the British military became alarmed at the possibility of a French invasion. They got further tunnelling banned in 1883, and the French gave up, disgusted at the stubborn British, who were so determined to keep their 'island fortress'. With the key position of Ashford within the SER network, as well as the skills in the railway works, the potential lost through military short-sightedness was incalculable. At last, in the 20th century, Ashford did garner considerable advantage from the Channel Tunnel - but the railway works had already closed!

I've been through, have you?

Overture Service 1994   le Shuttle

Eurotunnel Brochure 1994   ZZZ00284

The South Eastern Mechanics Institute had a very high profile visitor in 1855: Charles Dickens. He came to give a reading from his latest novel, 'A Christmas Carol', to an appreciative audience. Wilkie Collins, later the author of 'The Moonstone', accompanied his friend, but whether he gave any reading is not known.

Dickens was not the only prominent visitor to Ashford during this period. HRH Prince Alfred, the Duke of Edinburgh, second son of Queen Victoria, leased Eastwell Park

EASTWELL PARK c1865 7080

from the Earl of Winchelsea at the time of his marriage. His wife was Grand Duchess Marie Alexandrovna, a daughter of Czar Alexander II of Russia. They entertained many friends and relations at their home, including the Prince and Princess of Wales (later Edward VII and Queen Alexandra), and other European royalty. They lived here until 1886. Another visitor was a young naval officer trained by the Duke, who went on to be very successful in his career, Prince Louis of Battenberg. Prince Louis rose to the top of the Royal Navy, but was obliged to step down as a result of anti-German bigotry during the First World War. Prince Louis' son, Lord Louis Mountbatten, visited Ashford many times to be with his daughter (now Countess Mountbatten), whose home is at Mersham.

EASTWELL PARK, THE TOWERS c1960 E164071a

The magnificent gateway to Eastwell Park, where Queen Marie of Romania, daughter of the Duke of Edinburgh, was born. This formal entrance is not used as such any more.

Russian Princess and Romanian Queen

Born at Eastwell in 1875, Princess Marie was a daughter of the Duke of Edinburgh and his wife, a Russian princess. At seventeen, she married Ferdinand Hohenzollern, Crown Prince of Romania, and later became Queen. Moving to Romania, she immersed herself in Romania's affairs. Among her particular projects was the Summer Palace at Sinaia, which she had decorated mainly in Art Nouveau style, but with touches of Byzantine and Celtic styles as well. In 1995 a group from Ashford Borough Council visited Sinaia during a tour to see what links could usefully be developed with nearby Brasov . A guide at the palace explained that Queen Marie is very highly regarded in Romania today. Naturally, when the Eastwell connection was explained, the Ashford party were proud and delighted. Among other achievements, Queen Marie informally attended the Paris Peace Conference after World War I, where her lobbying assisted the Romanians to get a better result from the settlement.

The Summer Palace at Sinaia, Romania 1995 S14571 lk (Les Lawrie)
Members of the delegation from Ashford can be seen in the foreground, including Councillors Apps and Weatherall.

The St John's Ambulance Association was founded in 1877 by John Furley, who was born in North Street. Its main purpose was training people in first aid, which was to be administered until the professionals arrived. Furley had earlier been one of the prime movers in the establishment of the British Red Cross Society in 1868.

Clearly he was able to impress the royal admiral living at Eastwell enough to get his active support: the Duke of Edinburgh agreed to be the President of the local St John's

Ambulance in 1879. The Ashford Corps is the oldest surviving member unit of the St John's Ambulance anywhere. Furley took his first aid activities seriously; he designed a litter, a sort of hand-propelled ambulance for carrying patients. This was built locally, and called the Ashford litter.

The general population of Kent at the end of the 1800s was about four times what it had been at the beginning. This increase would have been in the towns, since the countryside was becoming depopulated, with fewer and fewer people working on the land. Ashford's population increased from 2,151 to 12,808, an increase of almost six times. However, the difference in the population growth from Kent as a whole can be seen to be due to the employment from the railway.

THE MASONIC HALL AND TEMPLE, NORTH STREET 2004 A71712k (Les Lawrie)

This house in North Street, where Sir John Furley was born, now houses the Masonic Hall and Temple. The passer-by is Robert Blount, walking home.

Godinton Road was built as part of the general expansion in late Victorian times.

This almost organic growth in population had to be housed somewhere in Ashford, and so there was additional building in various parts of the town. Among these are areas just north of the town centre, and along Godinton Road towards Great Chart. Nearby villages, such as Willesborough and Kennington, also experienced some of this additional growth, and were rapidly changing into suburbs of Ashford.

There was an increasing realisation in the whole country that proper provision had to be made for the rapidly increasing population. Some measures, such as improvements in healthcare and sanitation, by decreasing the death rate, actually made the housing problem worse. We start to see good works done in an organised way early in the century, rather than in the former haphazard efforts of local philanthropists.

We know that a National School existed before 1816, because the school had to move to Gravel Walk in order to accommodate the increased numbers of pupils attending. These schools were long tied very closely to, and organised by, the established church. Nonconformists established their own school by the late 1830s, probably in New Rents.

GREAT CHART, THE VILLAGE 1901 47551

This view looks down the hill from the church. The windmill has since been removed.

Education was not compulsory for all children until 1870.

An example of organised work for community benefit can be found in the reconstruction of the road bridge over the river Stour in 1834; clearly, it could no longer cope with the traffic it was expected to take. It would be rebuilt twice more before the end of the century. It seems that local archaeologists were able to make a study of the site, because they reported finding ancient artefacts and evidence of prehistoric activity low down in the river banks of a ford across the river. Presumably they were looking for the ash-ford, and believed they had found it!

Did you know?
There is a Ford in Ashford

The land is built up high on either side of the river at the points where main roads would have crossed in bygone days. It is difficult to envisage a ford there. However, there is still one ford within the town. Beaver Lane used to meander around South Ashford, eventually to emerge on the Great Chart road after crossing the Great Stour near Chart Leacon. This ford can still be seen with its approach roads close to Brookfield Road.

WILLESBOROUGH, THE LEES 1909 61559

This part of Willesborough still marks the edge of the urban area of Ashford.

Local government, where there is some element of democratic local choice, can be traced back in Ashford to 1824. This was when the first improvement commissioners were elected.

Their responsibilities were the watch, lighting and paving. Safety concerns were addressed by the watch, who were the first organised policing, with an element of public control. Watchmen had very limited powers, and their main impact was as a deterrent to bad behaviour. Street lighting was established with the installation of oil lamps, though these were replaced around 1832 with gas lights, giving a better light. These would eventually be replaced with electric lighting, which did not require the attentions of a lamplighter.

The paving of roads and footpaths continued all through this period, and well into the 1900s. The nature of the work would gradually change from installing the paving to simply maintaining it, though some roads, such as Mace Lane, remained unpaved until the 1970s.

By stages the nature of local government changed throughout the 1800s. A local government board, with 21 members, was set up in 1863, which was itself superseded by an Urban District Council in 1894. Each change would be accompanied by changes in powers, and many more responsibilities

THE COTTAGE HOSPITAL 1908 60335

being added over the years. Party politics became established in the local area through these various democratic institutions, including the creation of a seat in Parliament for Ashford in 1885. The holding of this seat was to fall to Conservative and Unionist members, almost without exception.

Some of what are now regarded as essential public services were provided through public subscription or private donation. Collections were made to raise the money for a hospital, and this opened in Station Road in 1870. The local newspaper credited John Furley with the idea and much of the collection of funds. This hospital was replaced by the Cottage Hospital in Hardinge Road (60335), donated as a memorial by one of the Burra family, supporters of several public causes in the town. This hospital served Ashford for over 50 years until well into the 1900s, when it was replaced by Ashford Hospital. The building is now put to many uses, including offices and a day centre.

Later in the 1800s, other services were provided by public authorities. A new sewage works was opened in 1883, a reservoir and water tower was completed at Barrow Hill in 1897, and another reservoir, with a capacity of 280,000 gallons, was opened at Henwood the following year. All of these have been replaced with larger and more modern facilities elsewhere over time.

Where do we Put the Body?

A train journey from Ashford to London can remind you about the Victorian fascination with death. Close beside the line is a vast necropolis. If you wanted to visit one particular grave, finding it might have been difficult. However, most cemeteries, like the one in Canterbury Road, were organised so that one part was especially for Roman Catholics, for example. The Canterbury Road cemetery was even more organised than that, though. If you walk around the paths, you may wonder why there appear to be two rather large traffic roundabouts. They are all that remains of two chapels, which were used for burial services when the cemetery was first created. The larger one was for use by the Church of England, while the other was for use by nonconformist churches. The appearance of the chapels can be seen from the lodge by the gate, which was built in the same Gothic

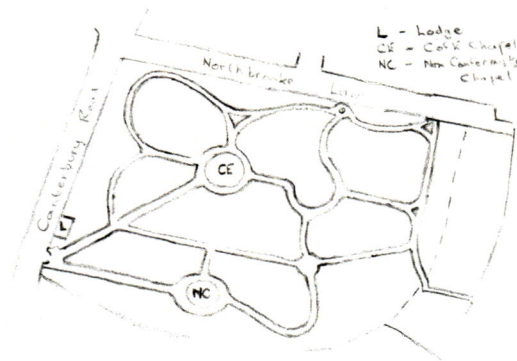

Diagram Map of Canterbury Road Cemetery ZZZ00285
(Les Lawrie)

THE VIEW FROM THE RECREATION GROUND 1901 47519

One lasting legacy to the people of Ashford from this late Victorian era of public works for the social well-being of the townsfolk, is Victoria Park (see above), the largest open recreational space within the town. The land for this was bought in 1898, in order to create a public park from the land previously leased as playing fields. Recent development has started to reduce the open area. The Hubert fountain (page 65), which now dominates much of the park, was at this time in the grounds of Olantigh, Wye. It had first appeared as an exhibit in the Second International Exhibition of 1862 in the Royal Horticultural Society gardens, London. The fountain has been restored, and now works again after many years of neglect. The stags have been removed, however.

The church has long played a significant part in the life of the town of Ashford, and especially St Mary's. In the 1800s, the congregation was growing so much that it was necessary to widen the church aisles in 1827. The north and south galleries were also moved, though apparently not enlarged. With galleries the size they are now, but much closer together, the interior must have been very dark, with few able to see what was going on. However, the congregation continued to expand, so that the parish church had to be lengthened by an extra bay.

This expansion started in 1860. The parish also included that part of the town south of the railway, so the consecration of Christchurch, in 1889, was a further part of the pattern. These changes in the church serve to confirm the growth of the town. They have left Ashford with a very capacious church, sometimes called 'the Little Cathedral of Kent'.

VICTORIA PARK, THE FOUNTAIN 1921 70312

THE PARISH CHURCH FROM THE NORTH WEST 1928 80982

This illustrates the extensions to the parish church. The small tower was originally on the outside main wall, and the most westerly window was added with an extra bay.

Other denominations also moved into new, or larger, town centre premises during this time. The Congregational church opened in Tufton Street, and the Roman Catholic church (below) opened at Barrow Hill, both in1865. The Methodists opened their Bank Street church in 1875, while the Baptists combined congregations and built the Station Road church in 1881. The Quakers acquired a meeting house in Hempstead Street during 1898. These were merely the developments in the town centre; other suburbs also had their own new churches.

The oldest surviving registered company in Britain was set up in January 1856 at a meeting of farmers in the Saracen's Head. The Ashford Cattle Market Company still runs the livestock market, even though it moved from its Elwick Road site to accommodate the Channel Tunnel Rail Link. It now has modern facilities on the south-eastern edge of the town. Another institution related to agriculture was set up just across the road from the market in 1861 - the Corn Exchange. This became for many years a venue for many of the town's social events, and its demolition was much regretted by local people.

THE ROMAN CATHOLIC CHURCH c1908 60333

St Teresa's Church has since been replaced with a church of a striking modern design. Western Avenue, shown here, no longer joins Maidstone Road.

THE LIVESTOCK MARKET 1906 53445

NORTH STREET 1950 A71019

The building on the left with the North Street sign is the Saracen's Head Hotel, with the public house known as the Shades just beyond it.

KENNINGTON, THE MILL 1901 47543

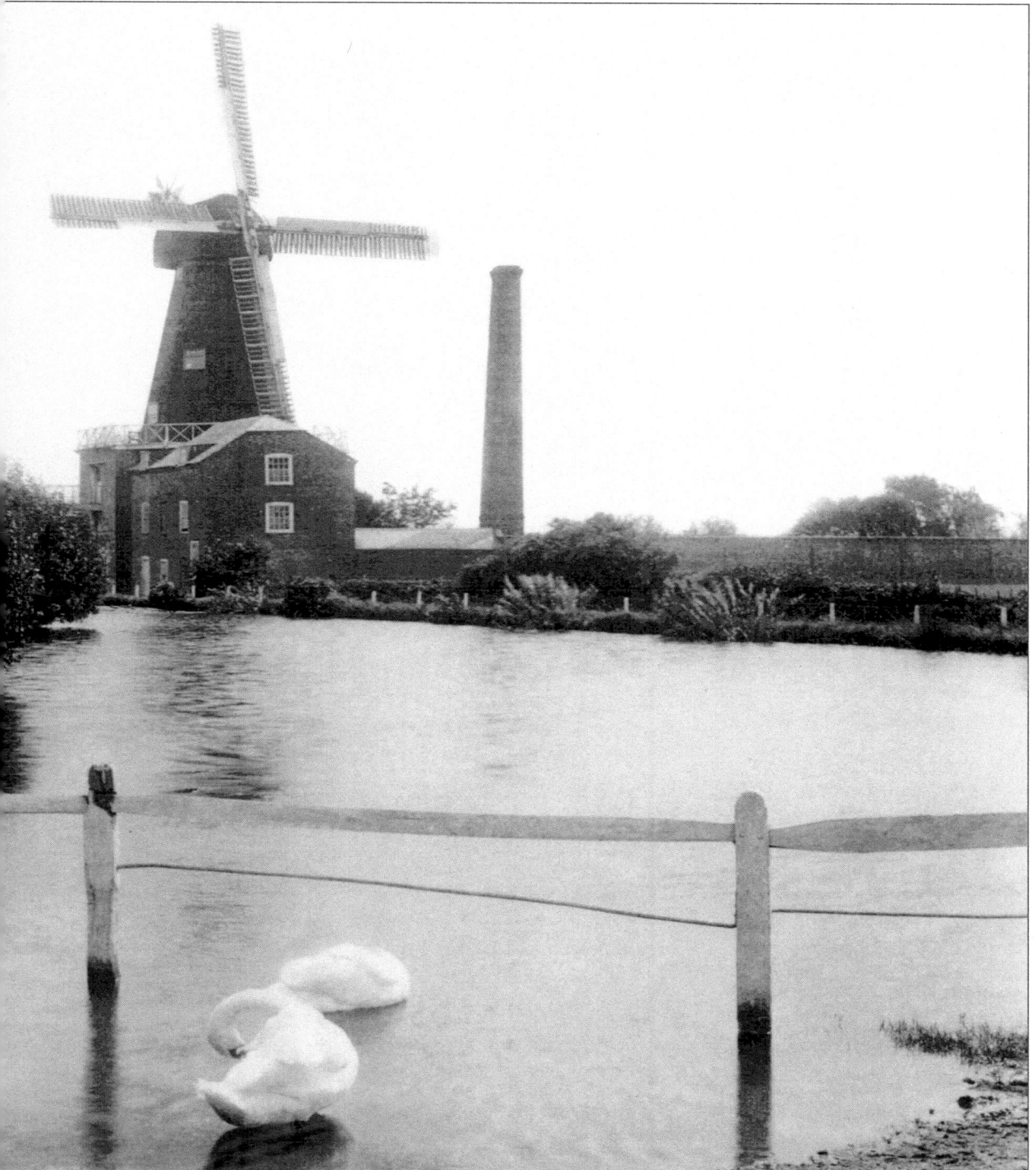

In any period of history, prominent buildings will be removed from any town. Some of these will be a loss, others will hardly be missed at all. Ashford's original manor house was on the site of the Saracen's Head, which was demolished in 1862 and replaced with a new Saracen's Head Hotel. One of Ashford's mills, a smock mill in Regent's Place, was dismantled and moved to the village of Badlesmere. Kent's windmills such as this were essentially temporary wooden structures. Those which survive are exceptions to the rule: we may be thankful that Willesborough windmill is one of them (see above, and also page 84).

WILLESBOROUGH, THE WINDMILL AND THE SCHOOLS 1909 61558x

Willesborough windmill was restored to full working condition in the 1990s. The schools, now called Corne's Close, have been converted into specialised housing.

Ashford and its surrounding villages had many mills, mainly smock mills. Few survive, and those are mainly watermills, because of the their durable construction. There were mills at Great Chart, Kennington, Wye and central Ashford, which have all gone. Kennington's millpond has been largely filled in. The watermills at East Hill, Wye, Maidstone Road and Mersham are examples of survivors, though only Swanton Mill is anywhere near complete or able to produce flour from grain.

Not all businessmen and shopkeepers in the 1800s were honest and fair with their customers. It was not unknown for flour to have powdered chalk added to it to increase the profit margin. Weights and measures could also be adjusted, and not to the benefit of the customer. This led to the establishment of food retail businesses around Britain where the customers owned and controlled the shops, and thus the quality of what was provided. These Co-operative Societies were established in Kent, and an Ashford Co-operative Society was formed in 1888. This society continues to operate, although it has been through two mergers, and now forms part of the Co-operative Group. From its beginnings as a grocer's shop in Ashford, the Co-op now operates grocery stores, a department store, chemist's shops, travel agencies, a funeral business and a garage.

Another example of ordinary people getting together to try to improve their lot against what they saw as injustice was the formation of the Trade Union movement. One example is notable in Ashford: the formation of the Ashford branch of the Amalgamated Society of Railway Servants in 1889. These railwaymen were particularly incensed at the long hours they were compelled to work,

WYE, THE WINDMILL 1906 56962

Wye's windmill would have been endangered early, because of the competition with the watermill, which had a more certain source of power.

EAST HILL, PROVENDER MILL 2004 A71713k (Les Lawrie)

The sluice gates and spillway show how water power was harnessed. Provender Mill has been converted to a night club and public house.

and at their first meeting demanded that they only work ten hours a day for six days a week. The working week has now become somewhat shorter!

The establishment of the Trade Union movement, and the collective action of groups of workers, may have triggered a response in employers and businessmen. In 1901, businessmen in Ashford banded together and established the Chamber of Commerce to look after their joint interests. This is now a thriving business in itself, providing many services to the companies operating in Ashford and its surrounding area.

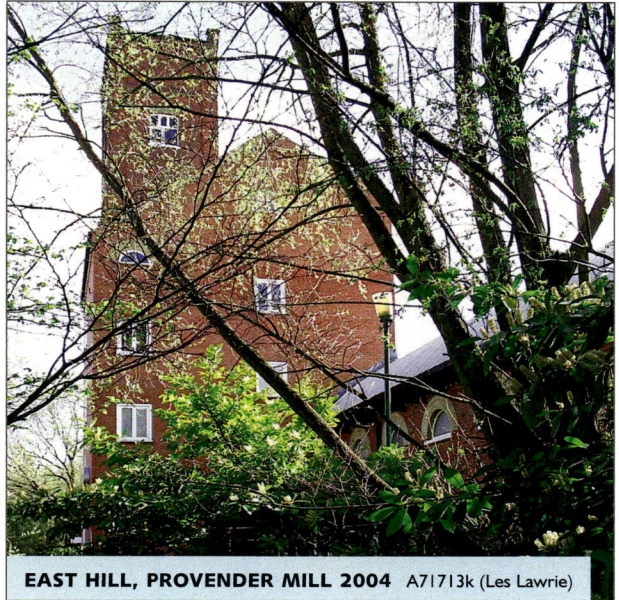

ASHFORD
Co-operative Society Limited
24 High Street, Ashford, Kent

SHARE PASS BOOK

Name MR. L. E. R. LAWRIE

No. 9251

This book must be retained by the Member and produced whenever a Deposit or Withdrawal is made. Interest on his account and bonus due will be entered in the Pass Book after the General Meeting of Members has so authorised. The date of this Meeting is published in the Society's picture Sheet.

INTEREST is calculated on the balance remaining in the account monthly.

LOAN ACCOUNTS. Members having the Share limit to their credit may make further deposits by opening a loan account.

THE AUTHOR'S ACS PASSBOOK
ZZZ00286 (from author's collection)

CHAPTER FOUR

Marching to Centre Stage

THE PEOPLE of Ashford welcomed Edward VII to the throne in 1901; some even knew him well, through his visits to Eastwell during the stay of his brother, the Duke of Edinburgh. They celebrated his coronation in 1902, as was the norm. Their main effort seems to have been saved for the mark of respect given on his death! Most businesses shut for the day of the funeral, all shops were shut, and even the public houses stayed closed for five hours across the middle of the day.

Ashford's business community was expanding throughout the 20th century, with new firms opening, and old firms expanding and relocating. One of the first new businesses of the century was the British Wheel Works in 1905, in what is now Mace Industrial Estate. They were wheelwrights and truck makers, and they were the largest such business in the country.

Headley Brothers' printing works, the Invicta Press (see page 77), suffered a major

WELLESLEY VILLAS 2004 A71714k (Les Lawrie)

Wellesley Villas would have faced the British Wheel Works. In one of these houses Marion Richardson, handwriting and art education pioneer, was born in 1892.

fire in their Edinburgh Road premises during 1906. This did many thousands of pounds worth of damage, so the company took the opportunity to relocate to their current site in Lower Queen's Road, a purpose-built premises. Much expanded, this firm continues to this day.

Hayward's cycle works, which had started in 1889, was going well and producing good cycles at this time. They had also expanded into motor engineering, a natural move during the infancy of the motor industry. They too suffered a fire in their New Street works in 1914.

The largest fire ever attended by the Ashford Fire Brigade was in 1903, when Olantigh Towers at Wye burned down - it was an imposing mansion set in a large park. During the rebuilding of the house in 1910, some items were sold. Within the park was the fountain exhibited at the Royal Horticultural Society; it was bought by George Harper, a local philanthropist, for the people of Ashford. It was set up in Victoria Park, and the water was turned on in 1912; but Harper did not attend the ceremony. Three weeks later he mysteriously committed suicide under a train passing through the Warren.

Military activity was continual throughout most of the 20th century. The reserve troops were becoming far more organised with the very real prospect of war, so in 1910 a drill hall was opened in Newtown Road for the local Territorial Army and to act as an area headquarters. Only four years later, the whole of Europe was to be plunged into a war that rapidly spread worldwide.

GOOD PRINTING QUICK DELIVERY KEEN PRICES!

PRINTING BOOKS, CATALOGUES & MAGAZINES POSTERS, HANDBILLS, PRICE LISTS, Etc.

STATIONERY FOR PRIVATE AND BUSINESS USE BY EVERY PROCESS

BOOKBINDING SINGLE VOLUMES OR ANY QUANTITY

ENVELOPES LARGE STOCKS HELD FOR IMMEDIATE REQUIREMENTS

PAPER WRAPPING PAPERS AND BAGS PLAIN OR PRINTED

HEADLEY BROTHERS

The Invicta Press (Lower Queen's Road)

44 HIGH STREET, ASHFORD, Kent

A wide range of Fancy Goods and Stationery

Gifts   Children's Books   Bible and Prayer Books

Agents for Peerless Brassware, Hornby and Meccano, and all makes of Fountain Pens

Telephone : Ashford 500

ADVERTISEMENT FOR HEADLEY BROTHERS 1951
ZZZ00287

Ashford, as a community in a strategic position, took a full part in the conflict. Volunteers joined the British armed forces, many giving their lives or their health. People at home supported the war effort through their work in key industries, some of which were based here. The British Wheel Works would have made many wheels and trucks for military uses, the railway works made and maintained rolling stock, and Pledge's Mills would have been working flat out to supply as much flour as possible to help feed the forces.

The railway changed their chief mechanical engineer at Ashford in 1913, when Harry Wainwright retired and R E L Maunsell was appointed. In early 1914 Maunsell authorised the building of 22 new locomotives, but they had to be built quickly. The design came from Wainwright, but it was modified by Maunsell in the light of experience from his previous railway. The locomotives were consequently built in two batches, one at Manchester and the other at Berlin; they were delivered during the summer of 1914, just as war broke out. The irony of these L-class locomotives is that the 'Germans', as the second batch were called, started their working lives pulling trains carrying soldiers, and military stores, to fight against their own makers.

Because of its strategic position near the channel ports, Ashford had troops billeted in townspeople's homes. Some troops were billeted in Church Road, Willesborough (below), including what is now the William Harvey public house. The scene in the photograph has changed little today. There was also a tented military encampment just east of Barrow Hill, round about where the Priory Motors garage is today. These could have been troops on their way to or from the battlefields of Flanders.

Some of those at home also became involved in the action. There were two air raids, though these had little physical effect on the town. Despite this, the effect on morale would have been considerable, especially in 1916 when the members of the special constabulary reported seeing a zeppelin (a rigid airship) go down in flames towards London.

Ashford citizens also took part in fundraising to help the war effort, and the

WILLESBOROUGH, CHURCH ROAD 1909 61560

scale of their success was recognised after the war. Towns that did well with fundraising were given a redundant tank in recognition of their success. Ashford's tank (see below) was driven into its final resting place, St Georges Square, in 1919. This Mark IV tank has since had its guns and engines removed, and for many years it contained an electricity sub-station. In recent years the Royal Tank Regiment have restored the tank so that it looks almost as it would have on its arrival. Other towns that received a tank have long since disposed of theirs.

Another memento of the First World War, now long gone, was a firing range in the Warren. The target machinery, which was worked from a trench in front of an earth embankment, provided

Why Call it a Tank?

The tank which Ashford still has on display is the Mark IV. This was introduced in 1916. It basically served as a mobile armoured machine gun post, since those were the weapons it was armed with. It could move up to enemy trenches in relative safety, and even cross some of the narrower ones (the ones up to about 10 feet wide). The official name for the armoured vehicle that we now call a tank was meant to be 'land battleship'. However, as a security measure against spies, they were shipped to the front in crates marked 'tank' - presumably it was thought that they would be assumed to be water or fuel tanks, rather than a secret weapon! The name 'land battleship', rather like the later German Panzerkampfwagen (literally armoured war vehicle), proved too complicated for soldiers, so the shorter name of tank stuck.

THE GREAT WAR TANK IN ST GEORGE'S SQUARE 2004 A71715k (Les Lawrie)

an irresistible temptation to boys playing in the area after the war. They would ride on the targets as others operated the levers to raise them. Not all military things left behind gave such innocent fun. One boy from the Hills family picked up a small object near Barrow Hill only for it to explode - it was a detonator, and he lost several fingers as a result.

World War I was referred to as 'the war to end wars' by many because of the horrors of modern warfare that they experienced. People were determined that those who died would be remembered, in the sincere hope that it would help prevent another such war. To provide a fitting site for Ashford's memorial, the Urban District Council was presented with the Memorial Gardens, between Church Road and Station Road, in 1920. The stone cross memorial was erected in 1923, and written upon it are names of those killed in action during both World Wars. Other war memorials were set up around the town, including one in St Mary's Church. This carved wooden rood screen, installed in 1920, also has the unfortunate effect of cutting the church into two very distinct parts.

THE PARISH CHURCH, THE INTERIOR 1901 47530

Here we have an unobstructed view along the length of the parish church, before the installation of the rood screen in 1920.

Did you know?

An Early RAF Accident?

Not all military deaths happen in action, or as a result of combat. One young man died in 1921 at the age of 19: Fred Collins was a second Air Mechanic in the Royal Air Force when he died. He was buried in the Canterbury Road cemetery. Since the RAF was only formed in 1918, this may have been a very early aviation-related military accident. The R34 airship had been wrecked in January 1921 - was there a connection? It seems unlikely.

The acquisition of facilities for the use of the people of Ashford has left a fine legacy. 1919 saw the purchase of the old Grammar School building as a memorial to Dr Wilks, for use as a public meeting place. Ashford Urban District Council bought the area of land called the Warren on the western edge of the town during 1924 and 1925. This piece of woodland is valued highly by today's residents for informal exercise. The area has recently been added to by Ashford Borough Council's acquisition of some of Hoad's Wood. The land is maintained as woodland, with very limited built access ways.

Soon after the end of World War I, people realised that the Cottage Hospital was too small to serve the town effectively, and fundraising began for a larger modern hospital. By 1926 enough had been raised for the foundation stone to be laid, and this was done by the Duke of York, later to become King George VI. The source of the funds could be identified through the names of some of the wards. Tenterden ward presumably honoured its generous citizens, while Rotary ward commemorated the work of the Rotary Club. Southern ward was so named because of the money put into the scheme by the Southern Railway and its employees.

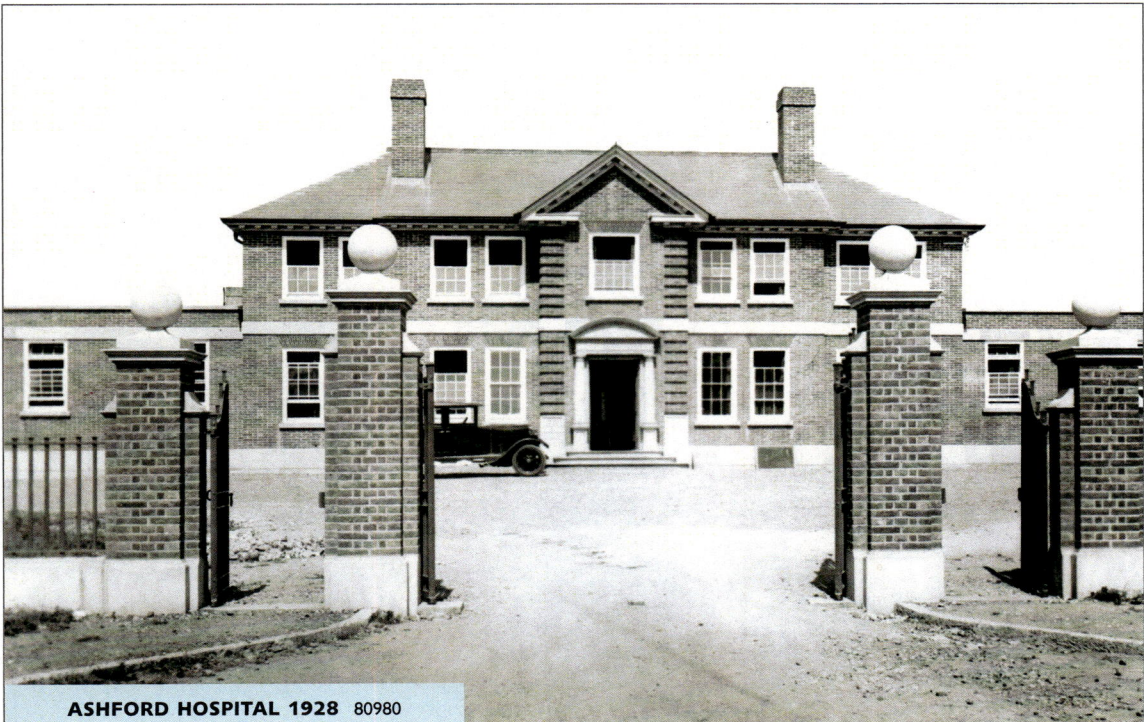

ASHFORD HOSPITAL 1928 80980

Ashford Hospital opened as a general hospital in 1928. Part was reopened as a hospital for the elderly in the 1980s by the popular actor Bill Owen (he played Compo in 'Last of the Summer Wine').

THE WHIST 2004 A71716k (Les Lawrie)

marketing of wool. Formed in 1920, Kent Wool Growers is the oldest producer-owned and producer-controlled co-operative. Their first base was in Dover Place, while their current home is in Tannery Lane - all of 50 yards away! The business has gradually expanded, so that it now provides for many needs of the farming community locally. In their premises is part of the original tannery, which has stood on the site for hundreds of years - it used to house the tanner's family. This house, The Whist (above, and page 83), is an interesting combination of a Queen Anne front part attached to a Tudor back section. Obviously tanning, though smelly, made enough profit for the owner to upgrade his house.

The Southern Railway had been formed through the amalgamation of three railway companies: the London Brighton & South Coast Railway, the London & South Western Railway, and the South Eastern & Chatham Railway. The Chief Mechanical Engineer of the SECR became CME for the Southern Railway - R E L Maunsell continued in this post until 1938, and was responsible for the railway works at Newtown. He lived in Canterbury Road.

The railway was not the only business in Ashford to see major change in the inter-war years. Local farmers got together and formed a co-operative for the collection and

Another co-operative business had an exciting change to their High Street premises in the year of the General Strike, 1926: they were destroyed by fire. Ashford Co-operative Society's store provided what was probably the most well known fire to be dealt with by the Ashford Fire Brigade, mainly because it was where everybody could see it - right on the High Street. The store was rebuilt on the same site (A71065a, on page 83, the building with the clock), and the new store is still a department store today.

THE WHIST 2004 A71717k Les Lawrie)

LOWER HIGH STREET c1965 A711065a

Hayward's received a rival in the cycle building business in 1923 when Norman Cycles opened their factory in Beaver Road. Norman's built bicycles and motorcycles in Ashford until 1961; some of the motorcycles were very highly rated by leading racing riders. Norman enthusiasts still gather with their machines regularly at Willesborough windmill.

Politically speaking, the inter-war years were turbulent times for Britain, with the Depression and the rise of Fascism and Nazism. Many were expressing their grievances through direct political action. During the General Strike, Ashford was considered one of the top grade towns by the Trades Union Congress, because such a high proportion of trade unionists locally took part. The main employer in the town, the railway, was very highly unionised.

In Ashford an ancient grievance was the root of one of the most unusual political upsets of the 20th century: in the General Election of 1929, the people of Ashford returned a Liberal MP. This was largely because of tithes, for the Rev Roderick Kedward supported moves to reform taxes based on the amount produced from a piece of land. This was a popular cause in the rural areas, where farmers considered these tithes one burden too many in hard times. This was the only break in a procession of Conservative and Unionist MPs to represent the Ashford constituency. A memorial to Kedward was moved from Hothfield to the Ashford Cattle Market when it re-located to Orbital Park in 1998.

WILLESBOROUGH WINDMILL 1965 A71082

This windmill was compulsorily purchased later by the Borough Council when the repairs required under a listed building notice were not carried out.

The Urban District of Ashford was reviewed in 1934, when Kennington and Willesborough were included.

This recognised the reality that the town was expanding, and led to an instantaneous population rise of several thousand. This change meant that the urban area was administered by a single local council. Today's Ashford Borough Council covers all the current urban area of Ashford, but also almost 200 square miles of rural Kent around it. The differing needs of urban and rural dwellers lead to some difficult choices having to be made, something which was not faced by the councillors of 1934.

WILLESBOROUGH, THE CHURCH 1909 61563x

There is little green space so close to Willesborough church now.

Ashford became something of a training ground for successful authors during the 20th century. Some have used local knowledge to enhance their work. One of them is Dudley Pope, famous for his maritime novels, who was a pupil at Ashford Grammar School. He used at least one local story, which he must have heard as a child, about the announcer at Ashford Station: '... he had most fun with the little two-carriage train waiting on the other side of that platform for passengers. It went to Canterbury, calling at Wye, Chilham and Chartham (whose first two letters were pronounced as they were in Chatham and Chiswick), but the porter was already having

his regular joke, crying out to the few people on the platform that the little train was for 'Why kill 'em and cart 'em to Can-ter-bury ...' Clare had a feeling that the old porter and the joke dated back to the opening of the branch line.'

H E Bates, now most famous for the televised adaptation of his 'Darling Buds of May', was very much a local resident, setting many of his novels in the countryside nearby. Noel Coward had a house in nearby Aldington. When this was sold to a builder, a tale was told of one room being wallpapered with music manuscripts. Taking into account Coward's reputation for flamboyance, this does not seem particularly surprising. More recently there has been Frederick Forsyth, who started his professional career by writing with the local newspaper. He went on to work for the BBC; he was a war correspondent during the Biafran war, where his experiences gave him material for his best-selling novel 'The Dogs of War'.

Among Ashford's writers was the eminent French philosopher Simone Weil, who is considered one of the greatest philosophers of the 20th century. She escaped from France after its defeat during the Second World War, but felt almost guilty about this. She was determined to suffer as she believed the people of France were suffering, and so she lived on what was effectively a starvation diet. She became extremely ill, and died in 1943 in the Grosvenor Sanatorium, Kennington.

The Second World War saw Ashford very much more in the actual front line than ever before. Always in a strategic position, the

KENNINGTON, THE GROSVENOR SANATORIUM 1921 70320

Grosvenor Hall used to be a sanatorium; here Simone Weil, the great French philosopher, died during World War II. Later, Grosvenor Hall became a training college for young police officers from many forces.

town was now a target for bombing raids, and on a direct line to London. Several streets were bombed, including Kent Avenue and Hardinge Road, which suffered significant casualties. Despite being a prime target, the railway works suffered hardly at all; the workers were more concerned about the hole in the roof causing them to get cold and wet.

Ordinary families were encouraged to have their own air-raid shelters, depending on the amount of space they had. If they had a garden, they were encouraged to build Anderson shelters, tunnels of corrugated iron sheet covered with earth. If there was no garden, they should make a Morrison shelter,

a structure rather like a table made of steel. How valuable these shelters were in saving life is rather doubtful, but they certainly gave a feeling of protection. Large institutions like schools had much more strongly built shelters. St Mary's school shelters were under the playground, with strong walls and a concrete roof. The site was eventually covered with a new building for the school.

The North Boys' School shelters were under their playing field, and for many years their location was forgotten. They were rediscovered in the 1990s during the building of an extension to the main building. The excavator digging the foundations broke through the concrete roof into the void below. The shelters were a pair of long narrow chambers, perhaps 40 feet long and 8 feet wide. They were constructed with concrete walls about 5 feet high and a concrete roof, over which a layer of earth had been placed. So that the new foundations could be laid quickly, the shelters were filled in completely. The whereabouts of the shelters for the North Girls' School are also forgotten by the authorities, though they may be underneath a car park, waiting to be discovered accidentally by some other unsuspecting developer.

Shelters were only of value in the case of a bomb blast some distance away; a direct hit, or even a close miss, could still wreak considerable damage. Luck, good or bad, could play an important part in what damage was done and who was injured. The Roman Catholic school was destroyed by a V1 (popularly known as a Doodlebug - an early guided missile), which landed and exploded very close to the school buildings. However, the school day had ended, and everybody had gone home!

Numbers 15 and 16 Barrow Hill Cottages were destroyed when a German aircraft was shot down, and crashed into the houses. The scarring caused to the building by the still turning propeller could be seen on the stonework until the cottages were rebuilt after the war. There are too many stories of heroism, good luck, bad luck or just plain odd events from this period for a general history to really do justice to them. So the reasonable thing is to let a sample give the flavour of the times, as the civilian population experienced them.

Military activities in the area were also too numerous to report fully; however, some stand out. Various units were stationed in and around Ashford, and Eastwell Park was taken over by units of the Royal Armoured Corps. The extensive parkland gave them room to exercise their tanks, though there were times when they went out into the surrounding areas. One unit, from the Buffs, were training with secret weapons: these were Crocodiles, tanks converted to work as armoured flamethrowers.

Among the troops stationed there were Robert Runcie, later to become Archbishop of Canterbury, and Eric Lawrie, a veteran sergeant from the Royal Tank Regiment. Sergeant Lawrie commandeered the most secluded place in which to put his bed, an unused fireplace - the benefit of rank and experience. One time, when Sergeant Lawrie's tanks were outside Eastwell, they were driving down towards Canterbury from the Whitstable Road direction, when they encountered the ancient Westgate. The first tank wedged in the gateway, immovably stuck! Apparently there followed a lively debate on the options - to take the side panels off the tank, or to demolish the gateway. Fortunately for the heritage of Kent, the decision was to take off the side panels - not something that would have happened in the front line.

One group of volunteers from this area were officially a Home Guard unit, though they never paraded or stood guard duties.

These were Britain's 'Secret Army', a small group of men prepared for the day when there was an invasion of this country. They were trained as saboteurs and assassins, with the specific task of hiding until the invasion front line had passed by, then emerging and causing the maximum destruction and chaos. Special bunkers were provided for them in which to hide and store weapons and explosives. The entrances to some bunkers were disguised by such mundane things as animal drinking troughs.

The volunteers were chosen from people who knew the countryside and could survive in it most easily, people like farmers and gamekeepers. Among them was Peter Boulden, a member of a long-established farming family, later to become Mayor of Ashford twice. None of these men was expected to survive for more than 48 hours after they emerged from hiding, though it was hoped they could delay the invading army long enough for other troops to escape and regroup. One officer responsible for the Kent unit was based at Bilting; he was the brother of Ian Fleming, later a best-selling author.

WESTERN AVENUE c1908 60328

This view down Western Avenue looks towards Sackville Crescent, where the gardens contained dragon's teeth for many years.

For many years after the war, concrete structures littered the landscape; some were strong-points called pillboxes, and others were structures intended particularly as anti-tank defences. Some of these were concrete blocks about three feet high in the shape of a narrow pyramid, often with a steel spike embedded in the top. These were called dragon's teeth, and could be found in many places, especially where there had been a strong-point or road block. Dragon's teeth could be found alongside the Ashford to Maidstone railway line in Sackville Crescent, until the building of the Channel Tunnel Rail Link. These had been part of the defences for the town at the Godinton Road bridge over the railway - part of the bridge's parapet was removed to improve the field of fire. Fortunately, the bridge was rebuilt after the war - only to be demolished to make way for the Channel Tunnel Rail Link.

THE WARREN 2004 A71718k (Les Lawrie)

This concrete blockhouse would have guarded the railway line as it passed through the Warren.

Other dragon's teeth were used in connection with a strongpoint established in Headley Brothers' printing works. This was apparently built to look like an extension of the works. One story is that after the war the owner, Mr Pitt, instructed some workers to remove the dragon's teeth. On being asked where to put them, he indicated a nearby ditch. The ditch was duly filled with the offending concrete, and all seemed well. That is, all was well until there was a rainstorm, for water started to emerge in the middle of the works' cricket pitch because it could not find its way through the normal drainage ditch!

One pillbox that survives to this day is at Westhawk (see A71719k on page 90). It is a typical concrete pillbox (hexagonal in shape, with gun embrasures, and sunk half below ground level), but built in an untypical location - the site of a Roman settlement. Roman towns of the 1st and 2nd century were fortified, so the Second World War fortifications would not have been the first on this site!

WESTHAWK 2004   A71719k (Les Lawrie)

One of the roadblocks constructed to control access to the town was in Chart Road. The main device for stopping traffic was a piece of bent rail, which fitted into a hole in the road and could be removed to allow traffic to pass. Part of the concrete structure for this roadblock still exists; many assume it is part of a retaining wall for the earth bank on which the old Ashford Hospital stands.

The 1945 Labour Government's first major impact on Ashford industry did not seem particularly threatening at the time: this was the nationalisation of the railways. However, nationalisation was to expose excess capacity in the system for building and repairing rolling stock. The Newtown works were neither the newest works, nor were they in an area with a chronic unemployment problem and thus requiring political intervention - Ashford had seemed to avoid the worst extremes of unemployment which hit other parts of Kent badly. There was therefore the threat, and eventually the reality, of rundown and closure of the works. This threat was to colour some political decision-making in the Urban District Council.

Professor Abercrombie, in his 1947 report to government about the development of the London area, considered other towns within reasonable reach. He described Ashford as the most suitable town for industrial expansion, because of its communications network. Despite his conclusions, Ashford was not designated a New Town. But by 1952 expansion was still on the cards, and other government legislation allowed towns like Ashford to expand without the formality of a New Town Corporation. Thus, late in the 20th century, the reason for the initial development of the Roman town still applied to Ashford - it is at a crossroads (albeit multi-directional and involving more than just roads).

THE NORTON KNATCHBULL SCHOOL 2004 A71720k (Les Lawrie)

Rebuilding and improvement of the town facilities began soon after the war's end. New buildings for Ashford Grammar School went up - they were originally built for about 400, but they have been expanded several times since. There are now about 1000 pupils in the school. The new buildings were opened in 1958. Lord Mountbatten of Burma, a war hero and also cousin to the royal family, performed the ceremony accompanied by his daughter and her husband, Lord Brabourne, chairman of the governors. Lady Brabourne was to become Countess Mountbatten in tragic circumstances when in 1979 her father was assassinated by a terrorist bomb in Ireland. Through the explosion she also lost her son

Nicholas, the dowager Lady Brabourne and a young local boy helping out with the boat. This, and the injuries she and her husband suffered, did not keep the Brabournes out of public life for long, even if they did have to attend the wedding of their son Lord Romsey in wheelchairs.

These new buildings left the Grammar School in a strange situation. Over more than three centuries, three sets of buildings were built and used, and all three were still standing, and in use, for some years. One set was a public hall, another was part of the neighbouring boys' secondary modern school, and the third is still used today by the school.

THE COUNTY SCHOOL FOR GIRLS 1908 60325

Other secondary schools had either been set up as new with new buildings earlier in the century, or, as in the case of the Girls' Grammar School (now Highworth School) they had moved from their original buildings to ones which were purpose-built for them. The first site for the County School for Girls was on the corner of Dover Place (see left) - none of these buildings still stand today. Moving to the Maidstone Road site (below) from Station Road allowed the school to take more pupils; Highworth School still occupy the buildings. Two totally new schools were built, however, after the Grammar School: The Towers School, on the northern edge of the town, and Duncan Bowen School, on the southern edge.

THE COUNTY SCHOOL FOR GIRLS 1928 80978

The Ashford Urban District Council met in the grand-looking building to the centre of the photograph.

HIGH STREET 1950 A71010

FLATS IN BYBROOK ROAD 2004 A71721k (Les Lawrie)

FLATS IN BYBROOK ROAD 2004 A71722k (Les Lawrie)

ELM PLACE 2004 A71723k (Les Lawrie)

One scheme to build houses more quickly and cheaply involved using prefabricated timber-framed panels. After a fatal fire, these homes received major remedial building work.

In 1959, London County Council, looking to re-house some of its booming population away from the capital, reached agreement with the Urban District Council for 5000 new homes to be built in Ashford, 85% being for London overspill. This started the really significant post war expansion. Most of what is now South Ashford was developed under this agreement, and so were smaller estates in Kennington and Willesborough. This served to integrate more fully parts of the town that were absorbed in 1934. The development in Kennington included Ashford's own version of high-rise flats at Bybrook. These were never a popular letting for tenants.

Some industry also moved out of London and other areas into what they saw as modern, spacious buildings in a pleasant semi-rural environment. Some smaller companies moved into the Henwood Industrial Estate, for example Burton Reproductions and Telemecanique. Other larger firms moved into purpose-built premises on the outskirts of the town, including Batchelors foods (still here, but now part of Campbells, A71724k, left, on page 98) and Proprietary Perfumes (also still here, but now called Quest International, A71724k, right, also page 98). Once both these firms were owned by Unilever, but Quest International is now part of ICI.

CAMPBELLS AND QUEST INTERNATIONAL 2004 A71724k (Les Lawrie)

Nationally, the motor industry in Britain was very successful in the 1950s and 1960s, thanks to many more people being able to own their own car. Overseas manufacturers were also making considerable inroads into the British motorcycle market. This had a negative effect on industries such as the cycle and motorcycle industry, with the result that many firms went out of production, including Ashford's own Norman cycles in 1961.

One local firm that started small and built into something rather large was Brake Brothers. This frozen foods firm started up in 1957 based in nearby Lenham, but as it expanded, it acquired offices in Ashford. Eventually the European headquarters were sited at Eureka Park in Ashford (see page 99), where the surroundings were very pleasant. This was at the time when the High Speed Rail Link was being built. At least one of the original brothers lived in the town. The company was eventually sold at a value of more than £100 million, and the original owners retired.

Professor Buchanan presented a report to the Government, outlining where the next major expansion of population should go. Among his proposals was that Ashford should grow to a size of 240,000 people by 1991. At about the same time that he presented his report, the Government realised that the post-war baby boom was over. This meant there was no need for a massive population increase, but they still accepted that a more limited expansion of Ashford should continue.

A further agreement with the London County Council allowed the District Council to develop another estate of about 1300 houses. This was again mainly for London overspill, and was completed in the early 1970s. Blocks of flats and maisonettes were built, with deck access to each dwelling; around the country, these deck access blocks have been deemed a contributing factor in many problem estates. These blocks in the Stanhope estate (photograph A71726k shows an example, on page 100) are now scheduled to be demolished and replaced with more socially acceptable housing under a Private Finance Initiative scheme.

BRAKE BROTHERS 2004 A71725k (Les Lawrie)

LUDDENHAM CLOSE, STANHOPE 2004   A71726k (Les Lawrie)

The visual quality of these 1960s and 1970s estates was not very attractive, though the accommodation provided inside was better than what was then available on the private market. At the same time, many new people were moving to Ashford from other urban areas, and wished to preserve its rural charm. This led to some lively planning debates.

HOPEWELL JUNIOR SCHOOL 2004   A71727 (Les Lawrie)

In the 1960s and 1970s estates, schools like Hopewell Junior School were also built. Fortunately the teaching does not reflect the boring, unattractive architecture.

Did you know?
NIMBYs and BANANAs

Ashford had its fair share of people who objected to development, which they saw as a threat to their neighbourhood. They wanted it to stay as they first saw it, but with more 'rural charm', not with added urban sprawl. Many of these protesters became known by the acronym that summed up their objections - NIMBYs (Not In My Back Yard). They objected to any development in their own immediate neighbourhood. A more extreme group of objectors emerged slightly later: BANANAs (Build Absolutely Nothing Anywhere Near Anybody).

Another early 1970s scheme to 'improve' the town was the development of the town centre Ringway. This reflects the almost god-like status awarded to the motor car during the late 20th century. The road was designed to keep large amounts of motor traffic moving freely into, out of and around the town centre. It became almost universally unpopular with inhabitants, and it also changed the character of the town quite dramatically through the demolition of houses, shops, pubs and business premises. Among the hostelries lost at this time were the Lord Roberts in North Street, and the Marlborough at the top of East Hill.

The final size and position of the Ringway, sometimes described as strangling the life out

STATION ROAD 1950 A71002

Station Road is now part of the Ashford Ringway, with traffic coming south towards us. Some traffic continues round into Elwick Road, while some exits towards the station.

of the town centre, was frequently criticised as ill judged, at the least! One councillor from that time described the process used to determine the route: consultation was carried out, and when the inevitable protest came in, the ring shrunk nearer to the town centre - this happened several times, until there was no room to shrink the Ringway any more. This has to rank as an all-time piece of political cowardice! Thus the town ended up with a road that used Somerset Road on the north side of the town centre, Wellesley Road and Station Road on the east, and Elwick Road on the south. Then it cut a swathe through various streets and houses back to Somerset Road. Most of these roads lost housing along one side or the other.

ELWICK ROAD 1901 47526

Elwick Road is now part of the Ashford Ringway, with three lanes of traffic going westward.

drive around some of the very narrow roads of Middle Row (see above). This part of the town still conformed to the medieval layout. Pedestrianisation of the town centre became possible, and was later carried out, cutting off half of Bank Street and the whole of the High Street from cars during the daytime. This allowed various civic and community functions to be organised right in the town centre in safety.

A considerable amount of housing was demolished to enable the building of the Ringway. Many residents mistakenly thought the demolition was to enable the construction of another controversial building, Charter House (A71728k, on page 104). Charter Consolidated was a large corporation with many mining interests, especially in Africa, and they built Charter House as a headquarters office block. Their designs were cut down at the planning stage so that the overall height was less than that of the parish church. A considerable amount of extra equipment has been installed on the roof of Charter House since then. The exposed and prominent position of the building has meant that few people can totally ignore it. Although many residents hate the building and cannot see any redeeming features in it, others feel it is a good example from the period, though not necessarily in the right place. It certainly has wonderful views and excellent facilities, including on-site car parking. Charter House has provided many people with employment over the years, and it has attracted semi-formal visits from such foreign dignitaries as Kenneth Kaunda, President of Zambia, to Ashford.

MIDDLE ROW 1908 60323

There were benefits from the Ringway, though many of these would probably have been achieved without it. The main road no longer ran through the High Street, and more especially through the very narrow Castle Street. The narrow East Hill was relieved of road traffic, allowing Ashford School to function with greater safety. Bank Street became the main vehicular access to the town centre, though it was still possible to

All of this area is now pedestrianised, with a performance area/bandstand sitting in the left half of the foreground.

HIGH STREET 1901 47521X

BANK STREET 1903 50331X

Traffic can still enter Bank Street, but the pedestrianisation starts at Tufton Street, which can be seen crossing just beyond the cart.

Perhaps to offset some criticism at the time, Charter Consolidated undertook a restoration project in nearby North Street. What was left of North Street after the construction of the Ringway and its associated roads was in a somewhat run-down condition. The company acquired most of the buildings and had them sensitively restored - several of them are of historical interest. The charming Knott's Square is one of the hidden gems of Ashford.

CHARTER HOUSE 2004   A71728k (Les Lawrie)

THE VIEW FROM THE CHURCH 1901   47520

This view along North Street shows the extent of development at that time. The Ringway now crosses about where the tree is, just to the left of North Street.

NORTH STREET 2004 A71729k (Les Lawrie)

Here we see North Street after the restoration done by Charter Consolidated. The buildings on the left include one where the sloping roofline can be seen through the top windows.

By the 1970s, Kent County Council had adopted a development plan for the whole county. The Kent Structure Plan continued the designation of Ashford as a significant growth point within Kent. This underpinned the continuing expansion of the town through the closing years of the 20th century, though KCC members were still willing to 'steal' some of the plums from Ashford when it suited their political purposes.

BEAVER LANE 2004 A71730k (Les Lawrie)

There had been a row of pre-war council houses in Beaver Lane; then foundations problems arose. The replacement homes are a good example of urban design.

PARK FARM 2004 A71731k (Les Lawrie)

Modern estates, like Park Farm, can look like very flat urban sprawl. Individually, the houses can be interesting; but the overall effect is a line on the horizon.

There was frequent criticism that incoming industries were encouraged to fill the KCC-owned former West Malling aerodrome, rather than to move to the more strategically placed Ashford. However, one American company rejected all blandishments, including grants in excess of £1million, in favour of the location that Ashford could offer the business. K'Nex, manufacturers of a particular type of construction toy, opened a factory in the town and ran the whole European arm of the business from it. They only moved when their parent company was taken over.

Not all Ashford developments have been promoted by local government; an example is the athletics stadium. A local athlete, Julie Rose, represented Great Britain and was considered to be a great prospect for the future. She was killed in an aircraft crash while studying in the United States. A memorial fund in her honour rapidly amassed sufficient funds to enable the building of a running track. A bid to the National Lottery fund jointly with the Ashford Borough Council (successors to the Urban District Council) was successful, and the Julie Rose Stadium was built. A much more comprehensive project than was originally envisaged, the track is of sufficiently high quality to host full international meetings - indeed, a Britain versus France match has already been held.

PROGRAMME FOR GB V FRANCE INTERNATIONAL ATHLETICS MATCH AT THE JULIE ROSE STADIUM 2001 ZZZ00289

In the meantime the fruits of the other labours of many of Ashford's leading citizens were being reaped. The Borough Council and many of the business community had supported the need for a cross-channel fixed link, particularly one that was by rail. They would prove to be one of very few areas in Kent to support such a scheme. The wholehearted support of a railway town, like Ashford, for a rail-based Channel Tunnel gained its own reward when an international passenger station was built in the town (see below). Initially, at least, there were only two, Ashford and London Waterloo.

THE INTERNATIONAL PASSENGER STATION 2004 A71732k (Les Lawrie)

The international passenger station can be seen across the platforms. A Eurostar train to Paris is just leaving the platform in the foreground.

Being less constrained for development space than the Waterloo area, Ashford International Passenger Station included considerable amounts of car parking. Some people, preferring to travel to France by train, but needing to get to the station by car, were attracted to Ashford, even from as far afield as Bristol. Struggling to the heart of London and then trying to find a secure parking space for their car was not an attractive option.

Being the first point that rail passengers from Europe could alight, Ashford became even more attractive as a business location. The journey times of two hours by train to the heart of Paris, and even less to Brussels, meant that the town was well placed in a European context. Business people wishing to be based in the UK, but with easy access to Europe, found it very convenient to be in or near Ashford. Similarly, some European businesses decided to relocate to Ashford, especially some French firms encouraged by Olivier Cadic.

At first the International Passenger Station was only open for Eurostar high-speed trains. These trains were designed to achieve speeds of 300 kilometres per hour, which they did on special tracks in France, and later in Belgium as well. The Government finally decided that there should be a dedicated high-speed line serving the Channel Tunnel in this country. Several different route options were suggested; the favoured one appeared to be alongside the motorway and through the sewage works. The Borough Council, in a remarkable display of unity across party political boundaries and between elected members and officials, campaigned for a route through the centre of the town and through the existing station.

THE DOMESTIC STATION 2004 A71733k (Les Lawrie)

The domestic station was also rebuilt at the same time that the IPS was built. It now has taxi ranks and bus stops right outside the door, and far fewer steps for passengers.

Their fear was that Ashford on a loop line could become a totally by-passed Ashford. The campaign proved successful once Martin Bryer, the Borough Technical Officer, convinced the Government that a town centre scheme could be achieved for the same cost as the favoured scheme.

A particular pleasure for the author was a trip he and his wife made by Eurostar while he was Mayor of Ashford. They took members of the 'Chain Gang' (the nickname for the gathering of Mayors and Chairmen of Councils) to Paris for a day trip, promoting the benefits of Eurostar and other forms of transport used that day.

Did you know?
Sounds an Odd Committee

During the early years of the Borough Council, one very minor committee seemed to accumulate members with themed names. In the chair was Councillor Merriel Carr; her deputy was Councillor Les Lawrie (pronounced Lorry). Other members of the committee at various times were Councillors Sid Ford and Jim Tugwell, while the person ultimately responsible for the minutes was the Borough Secretary, John Buss. The name of this committee? The Transport Liaison Working Group!

THE CIVIC CENTRE 2004 A71734k (Les Lawrie)

This building houses the offices and meeting place for Ashford Borough Council; it sits in one of the few remaining green spaces in the town centre.

CHAPTER FIVE

2000 to Infinity

FOR MANY years, Ashford has been the 'nearly town', but not any more! Ashford is at the heart of Europe, on the same footing as Paris, Lille, Brussels and even London. Facilities long missing from the town are beginning to appear.

There have been a variety of plans for Ashford's growth over the years, most of which were never fully implemented. The Government have now decreed that the population of Ashford will grow steadily over the next 30 years, with an extra 30,000 homes being built. These will give the population mass required to support many of the facilities that people would like to see, and which will enhance the quality of their lives.

Did you know?
Train for Everywhere

The specialised Channel Tunnel passenger train is amazing, and not just because of its scheduled stops in Ashford. Eurostar is designed to operate between three different countries, Belgium, France and the United Kingdom. The train is able to pick up power from a third rail system, as used in Kent, or from overhead power lines, and it changes smoothly between systems and voltages. Also its fire safety standards are higher than any other train in the UK.

How Many People will there Be?

The number of people in Ashford town has been measured by the National Census every ten years since 1801. The graph, which includes current projections, shows how the population has increased fairly steadily for the whole period. One exception, a sharp rise, is accounted for by the absorption of Willesborough and Kennington into the town in 1934. The Government forecast is that the number of homes in the south east of England needs to grow significantly up till 2030 or so. Two main reasons are cited. Firstly, the average size of families is decreasing, so a similar population to today's would need more housing units; secondly, there is a net migration into the region as a result of its economic success. Ashford was designated to accommodate some of that growth, about 30,000 homes. The forecast effect is also included in the graph, and appears to continue the smooth trend.

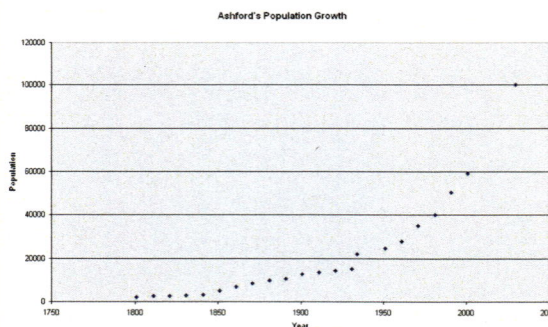

Population Growth
ZZZ00301 (Les Lawrie)

Did you know?

Exaggeration for Effect

During the discussion about expanding Ashford, various impacts were suggested. Some people were afraid of expansion, others opposed it. They feared that doubling the width of the town would give a population of 240,000 (400,000 at increased density); or that expanding out to include Wye would give a population of 300,000 (or over half a million). The planned population growth would move the edge of the town out by around 900 metres on average, but more likely by about 500 metres.

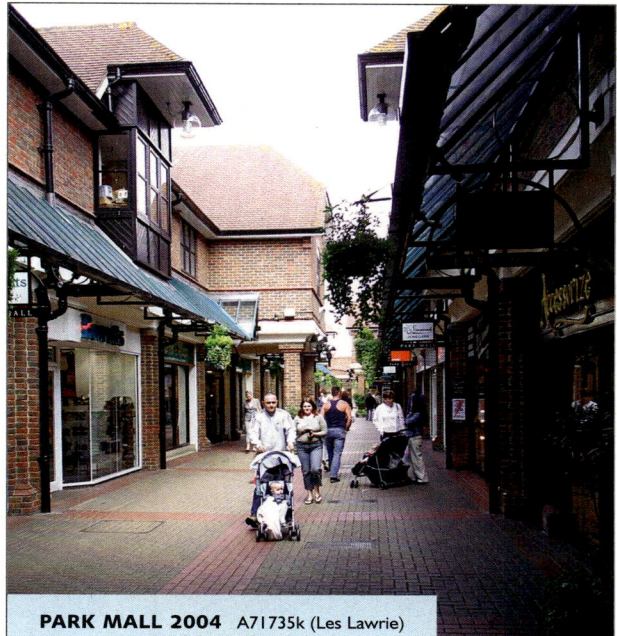

PARK MALL 2004 A71735k (Les Lawrie)

Shopping malls have not until recently been able to attract the top shops to take up their units, but now the potential rise in population makes Ashford more attractive to the big stores.

The multi-screen cinema operating at Junction 9 of the motorway came to the town after considerable negotiation, in which it was repeatedly stated that the population of Ashford was too small to support a facility like this. The ten-pin bowling centre was built because of the faith of its original developer in the future of Ashford. He had been involved in another scheme, which was aborted after considerable negotiation. The old railway station, which to many was outdated and unattractive, especially the ticket office area, has been replaced by a modern and interesting building. Nearby is the Designer Outlet Centre (A71736k, page 116), designed by one of the leading architects in Britain, Richard Rogers.

The white fabric roof structure covers over a hundred shop units, which attract millions of visitors each year. The roof, looking rather like a tented village from a distance, also excites much comment. The shop units sell discounted goods - last year's remaining stock and production overruns of top designer brands.

In 1908, in a book about Ashford parish church, Charles Igglesden wrote: 'The New Town and South Ashford are already joined and Willesborough has become a suburb. Another hundred years and Chart and Kennington may come into the clutches of the rapidly spreading town. Who knows? Another hundred years and the green patches and woodlands we now see around us may be sacrificed for serried rows of artizans' dwellings - when Ashford becomes the great commercial centre it promises to be. Who knows? Another hundred years, aye, in a quarter of a century's time, the tall chimneys of factories may rise out of the ground and challenge in height the old church tower upon which we stand, and, worse calamity of all, the fair country around us - the garden of England - may be honeycombed with coal pits and become a smoke-begrimed waste. Who knows?'

Well, we do know! Ashford has expanded, and the better things he expected have materialised, though the dwellings are not in rows. The factory chimneys, the coal mines and the smoke-begrimed waste are not part of the Ashford scene. A century of pessimism and gloom can now be consigned to the history books. We have much to look forward to, and Ashford has a way of coming through better than it was before.

What will we see in Ashford in fifty or a hundred years time?

Ashford will be a city with a thriving population. It will be made up of a network of communities connected together mainly by underground rapid transit systems, yet separated by corridors of green land along the traditional river routes. These communities will include Mersham, Kingsnorth, Shadoxhurst and Great Chart. The centre of the city will have much to make the quality of life pleasant

THE DESIGNER OUTLET CENTRE 2004 A71736k (Les Lawrie)

and attractive: a theatre, other entertainment venues, restaurants and other places to spend a pleasant evening. Most important of all, there will be people living in the centre, in apartments with views out over the pleasant old town area.

Because road traffic will have decreased over the century, many trees and plants will be seen in every street. Recreation centres, including gymnasia and swimming pools, will be found in each community, and many will have their own different specialised stadium.

Any short history of a town must necessarily be a selection of events and people from a much wider choice. I have chosen those I think are important, interesting, or just quirky. Ashford residents have been very restrained about their history in the past, so I am glad to do a little trumpet-blowing on their behalf. The picture used to be that Ashford had been nothing more than a sleepy little market town. I hope this book will go some way to changing that impression. Ashford was much more, is far more, and promises to become even more!

MILL COURT 2004 A71737 (Les Lawrie)

Mill Court is a small community, designed to look more towards the river and the footpaths leading to the station. Perhaps it is the first real 21st-century community.

Ashford must be THE town at the crossroads, a theme that recurs throughout its history. It is at another crossroads now, with so many possibilities for the future. Let us hope that the choices made are for the good of the town; but only history will tell.

Series of diagrammatic sketch maps to illustrate the development of the town of Ashford.

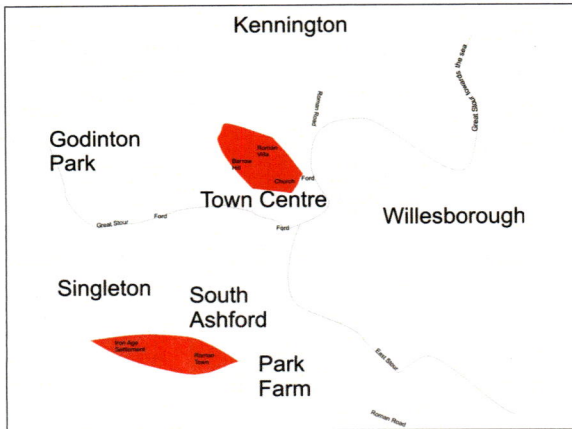

0 TO 400

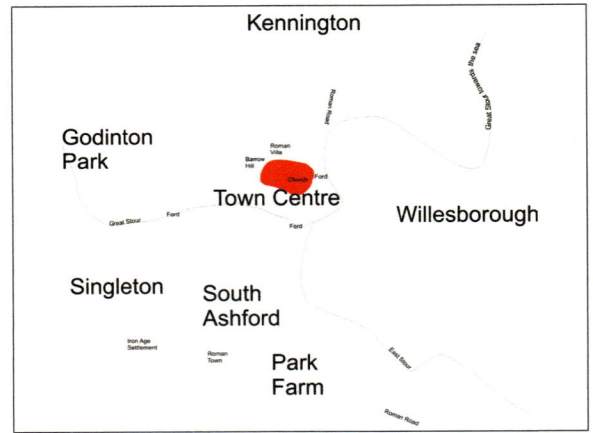

1600

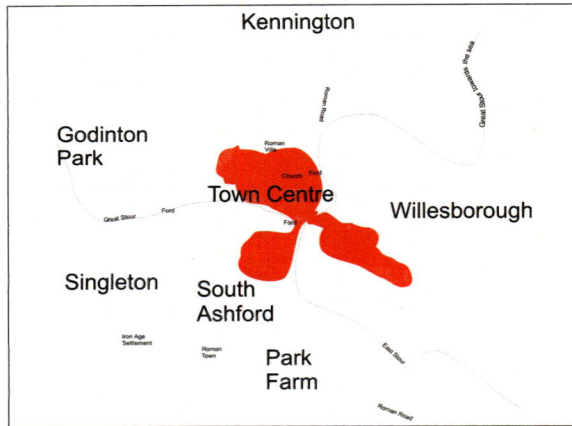

1870

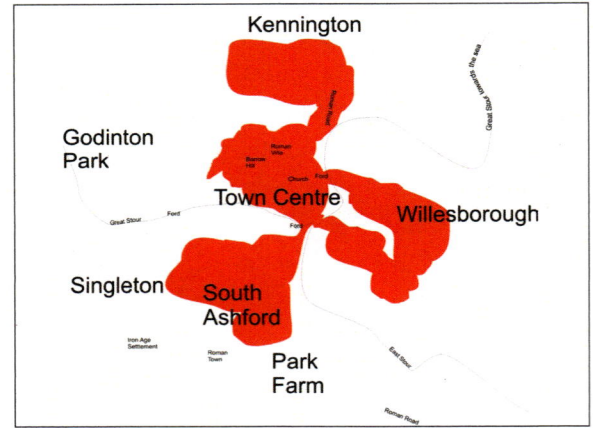

1965

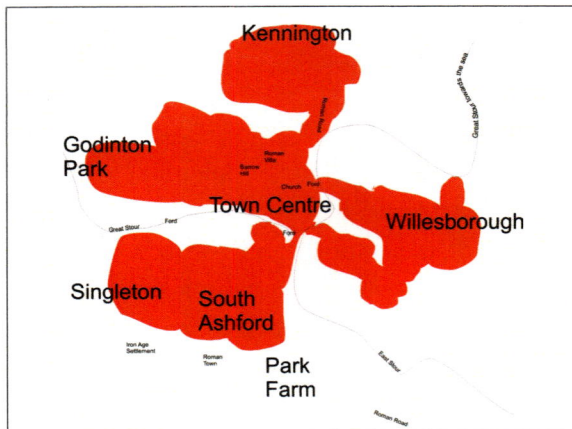

1990

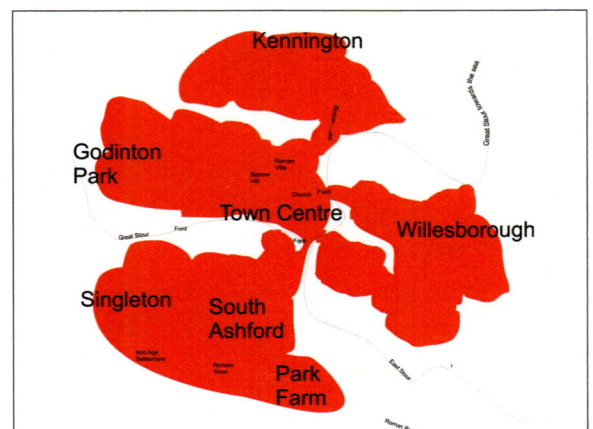

2000

Acknowledgements

I would like to acknowledge the support and help of my wife Jane from the outset to completion; also the encouragement of the dedicated Arthur Ruderman, and the infectious enthusiasm of Wilf Giles.

Bibliography

Books:

Arthur Ruderman: A History of Ashford

Arthur Ruderman and Richard Filmer: Ashford - A Pictorial History

Arthur Ruderman: The Personal Life and Family of Doctor John Wallis FRS

Simon Bagg: A Chronology of Ashford

Report of Excavation of Roman Settlement at Westhawk Farm

Philip G Dormer: Eastwell Park Historiette

Ashford's Past at Present, compiled by Ashford Local History Group

Gillian Draper and E T Mortimore: Lectures for the Friends of St Mary's Church, Ashford

W R Burden: An Illustrated Guide to Ashford Parish Church

Denise Bailey: Ashford People in the 1400s, 1500s and 1600s

Godinton Park (English Life Publications)

Gordon Turner: Ashford - The Coming of the Railway

Theo Barker: Shepherd Neame - A Story that's been Brewing for 300 Years

Brian Haresnape: Maunsell Locomotives

Dudley Pope: Convoy

Charles Igglesden: Ashford Church

Sarah Paynter: Roman Iron-working at Westhawk Farm, Kent (in cfa news, Spring 2002)

Anthony D F Streeten: Potters, Kilns and Markets in Medieval Kent - A Preliminary Study

J F Wadmore: Thomas Smythe of Westenhanger, Commonly called Customer Smythe

W W Rouse Ball: A Short Account of the History of Mathematics

Websites:

archaeologyse.co.uk

ccwf.cc.utexas.edu

fordham.edu/halsall/source

furleypark.kent.sch.uk/sirjohnfurley.htm

history.mcs.st andrews.ac.uk/Mathematicians/Wallis.html

homepages.rootsweb.com

kesr.org.uk/pages/history.htm

linkline.com/personal/xymox/roh/epes.htm

pages.prodigy.net

pinn.net/~sunshine/main.html

theotherside.co.uk/tm-heritage/background/tunnel.htm

users.globalnet.co.uk/~pstoog/trains/company/s/company_ser.htm

villagenet.co.uk/history

wye.org/history/

Media:

Ashford Adscene 23 April 2004

Meridian TV documentary

Oral History:

Brian Critchley

Wilf Giles

Tom Hall

Eric Lawrie

Harry Thompson